THEY WERE CALLED RECORDS, KIDS

THEY WERE CALLED RECORDS, KIDS

JAMES RODGERS

MoonPathPress

Copyright © 2018 James Rodgers

All rights reserved. No part of this publication may be reproduced distributed or transmitted in any form or by any means whatsoever without written permission from the publisher, except in the case of brief excerpts for critical reviews and articles. All inquiries should be addressed to MoonPath Press.

Poetry
ISBN 978-1-936657-34-6

Cover art: painting by Ryan Grey, titled *St. David*

Author photo: by James Rodgers

Design: Tonya Namura using Liquorstore Jazz (display) and Minion Pro (text)

MoonPath Press is dedicated to publishing the finest poets of the U.S. Pacific Northwest.

MoonPath Press
PO Box 445
Tillamook, OR 97141

MoonPathPress@gmail.com

http://MoonPathPress.com

I'd first like to dedicate this book to Shena Rodgers, my plus one at all concerts and events, and the one who has heard or read most of these poems more than anyone else, and still seems to enjoy them.

Next, my parents, Barb and Wayne Rodgers, for instilling in me a love of music, words, and a sense of humor.

I also want to dedicate this to my friends, especially Wes and Mike, for always being willing to listen to what I've just written.

Thanks to Ryan Grey for the incredible cover, and to Dave Russell for the chance to photograph some of his guitars and other pieces.

This book would not exist without all the singers, songwriters, and musicians who have inspired and entertained me over the decades, especially Tom Landa and Steve Mitchell, who are not only incredible musicians, but also good friends.

I also dedicate this book to Marjorie Rommel, who has always been supportive of my poetry, and pushed me when I needed a push.

Lastly, I want to dedicate this book to you, the reader, for without your eyes on the page, the music within would have no audience. Thank you!

Table of Contents

SET 1
They Were Called Records, Kids • 5
They're Mine! • 7
Music • 9
Still Spinning • 11
We All Want to Rule the World • 12
I Don't Just Listen • 13
When I Need a Hit • 15
Ladies and Gentlemen… • 17
Simple Pleasures • 19
Like a Statue in Dark Sunglasses • 21
Barracuda • 23
Despite the Tango • 24
Turntable Records • 27
Cinnamon Girl • 30
I Love That Song • 32
Better Than a Mud Shark Three-way • 34
The 27 Club • 36
Though Dylan Doesn't Help • 38
Mark • 41

HAIKU INTERLUDE • 45

SET 2
K-K-K-K-K-Kathmandu • 49
From the Jokhang • 50
Heading South • 52
Mikkelsen Harbor • 54
Southern Cross (Day 14) • 56
Octoberfest • 58
The One More Pint Band • 59
Dominique • 61
I Mean It, Dave, Stop It! • 64
I Can't Take It Easy • 66

HAIKU INTERLUDE • 69

SET 3
I'm Guessing Fool • 73
Thanks Mom • 74
I've Always Liked His Version Better • 75
Being From the West Coast Didn't Help • 76
Rain Tune • 77
J.C. • 78
Dave Brubeck, 3/12/06 • 80
Almost Jazz • 82
Channeling • 84

HAIKU INTERLUDE • 87

SET 4
Ponytail Beat • 91
Invitation • 92
Chile and the Crows • 94
She Doesn't Smile For Me • 96
Karen • 98
She's Gone • 100
This Song • 102
That Song • 104
I'm No Angel • 106
My Linda • 107

HAIKU INTERLUDE • 109

SET 5
The Opening Band • 113
Open Mic • 115
Aural Oatmeal • 116
Late Tuesday • 118
The Paperboys • 120
A Chance To Dance • 122

Encore • 124
Balance Due • 125

HAIKU INTERLUDE • 127

SET 6
The Song's Incorrect • 131
Blanket of Song • 133
Naked Support • 135
Everyone's A Critic • 137
Reading Billy • 138
Sing It, Sam • 140
Steve • 142
Sitting in the Car • 144
I Think I Love Her • 146
Song in My Head • 147
Oh Heavenly Day • 148
Long Way to the Top • 149
Always Drumming • 150
Just Listen • 151

HAIKU INTERLUDE • 153

SET 7
Can't You See the Tears? • 157
Fallen • 158
Bowie • 160
The Gospel • 162
P.R.N. • 164
No More Frank Zappa in This World • 167
George Jones • 169
From James to Jimi • 170
Out of the Garden • 172
He Was Our Man • 175

HAIKU INTERLUDE • 177

SET 8
It Better • 181
A Star Is Born • 182
Five Verses about the Park • 183
She Had a Growl • 184
Hers Was the Voice • 186
(I'm not) Walking on Sunshine • 188
Killer Star Tattoo • 189
Sara Hickman • 190
Everybody's Looking for Something • 192
Shining Star • 193
Madonna Behind My Eyes • 195
Emily • 196
Not Quite Dolly • 198
Anyone's Muse • 199
Lynn Marie • 200
What Are You Thinking? • 201
Karan Casey • 203
Kake King • 204
Patty Smith Is a Beautiful Woman • 205

HAIKU INTERLUDE • 207

SET 9
Arlo • 211
Dan Bern • 213
I'm Busy • 215
In Bloom • 216
His Music Is Still Timeless • 217
AC/DC Done? • 219
But Which Kind of Science? • 220
Not Thin • 222
We Can't All Be Dylan • 224
Stop Believin' • 227
No Discussion • 229
Morning Song • 231

HAIKU INTERLUDE • 235

SET 10
It's Too Late • 239
The Leafblower Symphony • 240
Sounds of the Sound • 243
Dream On • 245
Music Lover • 248
Big D • 250
Stop Writing Songs • 251
More Like a Steel Sieve • 253

HAIKU INTERLUDE • 255

ENCORE
It Won't Sing "Freebird" • 259
Artistry • 261

About the Author • 265

THEY WERE CALLED RECORDS, KIDS

SET 1

They Were Called Records, Kids

Most folks say
I'm far too young
to remember
Bill Haley and the Comets,
Little Richard,
The Big Bopper,
The Marcels,
The Penguins,
those early progenitors
in the creation
of Rock and Roll,
and I will admit,
I was created
more than a decade later,
but I love
the sound,
the urgency,
the innocence,
the true glory
of doo-wop harmony,
or Buddy Holly's guitar,
and I miss
the faraway look
in my mother's eyes
when Ritchie Valens
sang in Spanish,
or Fats Domino crooned,
his piano
lilting like a stroll,
about finding his thrill.
That right there,
like a musical IV,
these songs,

help keep me young,
even if they do
call them the oldies.

They're Mine!

The first two records
I bought as a kid,
back in the early 70s
when they were still called records,
were the debut release
from the Monkees
and the Jackson 5's *ABC*.
I was five
and I used my own money.
I wrote my name
in large three inch high letters
across the covers,
designating ownership,
destroying
all later collectible value
in the process.
I took them once
to a school dance
and it was easy
to find my records
in the stack,
the covers in perfect shape,
no bent corners,
no rounded edges,
or scuffed spines,
just my name
in black marker
across Davy Jones' face
and the Jacksons' afros.

I own
both recordings
on compact disc,

and will continue to buy them
with whatever new format
comes along,
my record player
resting quietly
under a layer of dust.
But I still have
both of those records
stacked in the closet,
not wanting to let them go,
partly out of nostalgia,
and memories,
but primarily
because I wrote my name
in permanent marker.

Music

Our family
owned an upright piano
for my entire childhood,
and yet,
I can't play more
than very choppy
Chopsticks.
I took two semesters,
Guitar 101,
then Guitar 102,
and yet,
still can't get my fingers
into the proper claw
to create a note.
I own a guitar,
a kazoo,
a recorder,
a Chinese three-string violin,
and a metronome,
yet the only music
that's colored the walls
of our house
is pre-recorded.
I listen intently,
delight in every strum,
every pluck,
every thunk,
memorize the words,
so I can sing along.
I may not have
a musical bone
within me,
cannot coax rhythm

from even
the simplest instrument,
and yet
when it comes
to playing audience,
I am a maestro.

Still Spinning

I'm not here
to mourn the vinyl record,
to write an elegy about it,
to fret over its passing,
as I believe
the reports of its demise
have been greatly exaggerated.
Vinyl
is alive and kicking,
resilient as ever,
kept alive by hipsters,
DJs,
and a giant wave of nostalgia.
Vinyl has outlasted
the 8-track,
the cassette,
the cassingle,
will likely outlast
the compact disc,
and will likely
still be around
long after the tiny chips
have been implanted
in our skulls,
streaming music
directly into our brains.
Vinyl
is the cockroach
of the music world,
and will last forever,
at least as long as
we keep it
out of the sun.

We All Want to Rule the World

Black circles,
grooved,
spun at thirty-three and a third
revolutions,
John's and Paul's voices
no longer in harmony,
their future
as a band
as blank
as the cover.
I was too young
to understand this
upon its release,
discovering them later,
after the split,
after the wives,
when cassettes were vogue,
and the revolution
long past.

I Don't Just Listen

The warmth
created by the friction
of a bit of diamond
against
the groove of vinyl
heats the room,
flickers up the walls,
swirls along the ceiling,
forces silence
down towards the carpet.
The vibration
of steel against plastic
tickles my nose,
my ears,
drops soft kisses
across
the back of my neck
and down my spine.
You enter the room,
give me
your usual
look of puzzlement,
mild disdain,
never understanding
why
I listen to music
so loud,
so distorted,
while standing
on a stepstool,
reaching towards
the heavens

beyond this dusty stucco,
smiling,
crying.

When I Need a Hit

For those days,
those weeks,
those times,
when the energy level
seems to be
nearing empty,
the mood clouds darkening,
there are certain songs,
musical adrenaline,
that I will listen to
as loud as possible
to pick me back up.
Either Patty Larkin's
percussive guitar work,
warning me
about the wolf at the door,
or INXS
and Jimmy Barnes
trying to tempt me
by extolling the virtues
of having a good time tonight,
possibly Prince
crooning over a slinky
hip-swiveling beat
about his love of mountains.
There's plenty more,
though these three
are my guaranteed power builders,
the guitar,
the bass,
the rhythm,
the words,
all reaching out

to lift me back up
where I need to be,
maybe even higher,
at least for a while.

Ladies and Gentlemen…

I was only four
when *Let It Be* was released,
the group disbanded,
solo careers begun.
I missed all of the mania,
hysteria,
shrill screaming,
and succession of singles,
the Ed Sullivan shows,
the movies,
the media exposure,
(or overexposure,
depending on who you ask),
the rumors of Paul's demise
just because
he was barefoot
on the cover of *Abbey Road*.
All of these moments
were discovered
a decade or more later, buried
treasure,
and while I feel
like I missed out
on so many
seminal moments
of music history,
now two of the four
no longer among us,
a Ringo solo tour
the closest I'll ever get, which
isn't all that close, their music,
their passion,

their playfulness,
their thirst of discovery
still tower over me,
a shadow
I'm willing to live in,
made brighter
each time
I press play.

Simple Pleasures

I've always been a fan
of simple pleasures.
As a child,
wet tennis shoes
on a tile floor,
three o' clock,
comic books,
*Chuck Berry Live
at the London Palladium*
on eight track,
static electricity,
Fluffy,
a quarter on the sidewalk,
and orange Nehi
were the things
that made me smile.
Now,
iced tea,
a pocket full of napkins
after spilling iced tea,
a sunny Saturday,
five o' clock,
dark chocolate,
a three minute pop song
with a chorus
I can instantly sing to,
a smile,
the sound of my wife's voice,
and the knowledge
I won't be in trouble
for mentioning my wife
in a poem
about simple pleasures

bring a grin to my face.
And I still enjoy
*Chuck Berry Live
at the London Palladium,*
except now,
I've got the compact disc.
Still a simple pleasure,
just a different format.

Like a Statue in Dark Sunglasses

I was ten,
maybe eleven,
when I got to see
Roy Orbison
live at a county fair.
I should have been bored,
hopped up
on soda pop
and cotton candy,
listening to an artist
my mother loved,
more than a decade
past his biggest hits,
a performer
who sat on a stool
the entire show,
didn't say
more than twenty words
to the audience
the entire night,
fourteen of those
being the quickly mumbled,
"Thank you"
he said
seven times
in two hours.
But I wasn't bored.

When Roy sang,
his voice
was a glimpse
into the heavens,
a tenor

so ethereal,
so obviously blessed
by a higher power,
even atheists
had to reconsider.
It's been
almost four decades
since that show,
hundreds of concerts
in-between,
and no other artist
or band
has held me
so tightly,
so close,
yet floating,
flying
so freely.

Barracuda

When Ann Wilson sang,
an alto in rock
considered by some
the wrong chromosome
for a lead singer,
I would turn up
my yellow plastic
transistor radio,
until the guitars
and her wail,
were all distorted fuzz,
and I'd jump
around the house,
much to my mother's chagrin.
Then the song would fade,
I'd roll the dial
back down to one,
and I'd wait
half an hour
or forty-five minutes
until it came back again,
swimming across the airwaves.

Despite the Tango

I was sixteen,
and for one week,
in P.E. class,
we were taught
different kinds of dance,
much to the displeasure
and disdain
of forty boys,
a few of the girls,
and Mr. Harrison,
who was also
the football coach.
Each forty five minute class,
for five days,
we were taught
a classic dance,
foxtrot,
waltz,
two I've forgotten,
and the tango,
which was on Friday.
The coach
picked everyone's partners,
to save time,
and on that day,
my fingers
were intertwined,
cheek dangerously
close to cheek,
with Jill Kopinsky,
a proximity
I had been dreaming about

for almost a year,
but was always
too shy to instigate.
Old records
amplified
over the P.A.,
echoing wildly
throughout the gym,
I was dancing,
clumsily,
with Jill Kopinsky,
the warmth
from her center,
tantalizingly close,
causing me
to slowly glow.
When the bell rang,
we unwound our fingers,
barely making eye contact,
our faces
slightly red,
from embarrassment
or exertion,
and my shower
in the locker room
was a bit cooler
than usual.

All these years later,
I still don't really
like to dance,
have no true urge

to get out
on a dance floor,
the music
and the rhythm
not a siren's call
for me,
as I don't particularly
derive any pleasure
from any kind of dancing,
except once,
for forty-five minutes,
nearly three decades ago.

Turntable Records

Ernie and I
don't always agree,
don't always see
eye to eye,
and it's not
just the height difference.
He cannot stand Sting,
rails regularly
against his voice
and lyrics,
while I believe
The Last Ship
was some
of his best songwriting
and singing.
I also tend to be
much more forgiving
of the later work
of Great Big Sea
and the Paperboys,
while Ernie prefers
their first two
or three albums only,
but we have plenty in common.
We both
still say albums.
We are both
passionate about music,
believe in its transcendence
and ability
to whisk us away,
far from here,
at least for a while.

I graduated
with a Speech Communication/
Radio Broadcasting major,
DJ'ed in high school
and college,
managed music stores
for most of a decade,
but switched to travel
eighteen years ago,
preferring to let music
be my hobby,
collecting it
on compact disc,
owning far more
than my house
should reasonably hold.

Ernie
runs a used music store
in the heart of Chinatown
in Victoria, BC,
his passion and knowledge
far deeper
than the thousands of albums,
tapes,
and CDs
that fill the shelves.
I see him
once or twice a year,
spend a few hours,
and low triple digits,
in his store,
talking music,
sharing music,

loving music.
I could never go back
to running a store myself,
and he can't see
how he could ever
do anything else,
but during those visits,
our passions unfurled,
appreciated,
open,
we can see
eye to eye,
especially
if neither of us
starts talking about Sting.

Cinnamon Girl

Her name was Carly,
and we dated
for just under a year
back in college,
our relationship ending
when she called
to tell me
she'd met someone else
during Summer break,
and although
it's been more
than two decades since,
whenever I
walk past a bakery,
or a restaurant
making breakfast,
whenever I smell
the scent of cinnamon
in the air,
I think of her.
Carly smelled like cinnamon.
She tried different soaps,
different perfumes,
but each time
the cinnamon girl came through,
as if it were
coursing through her veins,
great pools of it
just below
the surface of her skin.
She didn't like
rock-n-roll,

and hated Neil Young,
having been serenaded
by every boy she met,
that same song,
over and over,
every guy
thinking they were clever,
thinking they were the first.
Yeah, I sang it too.

I have no hard feelings
for her moving on,
my memories all pleasant,
warm and sweet,
but in the twenty odd years since
I've shied away
from cinnamon rolls,
opting for a croissant,
or a bagel,
breakfast options
with no emotional attachments,
no sticky history,
just pastries.

I Love That Song

I reached quickly
for the volume,
the music getting louder,
my voice rising up,
singing along,
singing harmony.
Song after song
poured from my radio,
and like a fountain of youth,
I was back
in high school,
dark gymnasium,
dancing, sweating,
hoping Kim
would say, "Yes,"
when a slow song played,
and just as my teen years
started to focus,
the DJ announced the call letters,
103.3, KOLD,
your oldies station,
and although
another song from my past
started to play,
I didn't sing along,
even though I knew
every word,
instead staring
into the rearview
at the crow's feet
around disappointed eyes,
wondering where

the time went,
wondering why
she never said, "Yes,"
to just one slow dance.

Better Than a Mud Shark Three-way

Dave Grohl had his
Rock Star Legend moment
when he fell
off a stage
in Gothenburg, Sweden,
broke his leg,
and finished the show.
Like Ozzy Osbourne
biting the head
off a bat,
David Bowie and Mick Jagger
caught nude in bed,
Keith Richards
snorting his father's ashes,
or Jim Morrison
exposing his privates
on stage
in Florida,
Dave's fall
elevated him
to the next level,
and unlike
all the other incidents,
was captured on video
for posterity,
and proof.
Looking at all
the other stories,
all the other legends,
just breaking his leg,
Dave got off easy.
Now immortal,

a Rock God,
with little
to no chance
of jail time,
rabies,
or an STD.

The 27 Club

Robert Johnson,
Brian Jones,
Jimi Hendrix,
Janis Joplin,
Jim Morrison,
Kurt Cobain,
Amy Winehouse.
All members
of the 27 Club,
forever 27,
their lives,
their music,
their trajectory,
all cut short
at the same age.
There are now
at least fifty members
of this elite Club,
but those seven
get to sit
in the back room,
behind the curtain,
smoke and laughter
drifting out
once in a while.

Though many believe
this Club doesn't exist,
just a fabrication
of the media,
Kurt had wanted in
so badly,

he'd told his friends
he'd be gone
by 27,
and put his head
on the business end
of a shotgun
just to be sure
the bouncers
would let him in.

As I near 50,
I've missed my chance,
(the fact I'm also not
a famous musician
a pure technicality),
but I do wonder
if there really is
a 27 Club,
how they decide
who performs each night,
and what age
do I have to be
for the Club
for poets.
My guess is
I've missed that one too.

Though Dylan Doesn't Help

I have a theory,
or at least
a strong belief,
that there are seven songs
in the known universe
of popular music
so well written,
so melodic,
so perfect
in structure
and tone,
they are bombproof.

I have heard
so many versions,
variations,
wild adaptations,
of each of these songs,
and they can't
be ruined.

Don't get me wrong,
many have tried,
muddied and stained them,
but the song
shines through.

I'm not saying
these are
the best songs ever,
or every version
is better than,
or as good as,

the original,
though many are,
or that every variation
needs to exist,
but in every case,
I'm so happy
to hear the song,
I don't care
if they rap it,
add a vocoder,
or let Bob Dylan
sing it.
It's still good.

The list is
(because I know
you've read this far,
and thought to yourself,
"I get it.
What are the damn songs!"),
in no particular order:
"Hallelujah,"
"St. James Infirmary,"
"All Along the Watchtower,"
"I've Just Seen a Face,"
"The Horses,"
"Satisfaction,"
"Unchained Melody."

Oh, I know,
you may not agree,
likely don't,
with some of these,

any of these,
but it's my list,
my strong belief,
my theory,
though I challenge you
to find a bad version.
I don't think
you can,
but I'd love it
if you tried.

Mark

Over the last fifteen years,
even though Mark
is in California,
and I'm in Washington,
we talk
about once every three weeks,
and whether I call him,
or he calls me,
he begins every conversation
with "Hey Peabo!"
The nickname started
when we both
worked in a music store
and I called
to leave him a message.
When the person asked for my name,
I said,
"Tell him Peabo Bryson called."
When Mark called me back
an hour or so later,
he said, "Hey Peabo!"
and that was that.

After he moved
back home to California,
back home
to take care of his mom,
back home
after the divorce,
I've only gotten to visit
three times total,
so all the weeks in between,

we call.
Most of our conversations
revolve around music, movies,
what we've been doing,
and politics,
and while we are both
on opposite sides of the middle,
we see eye to eye
more times than not.
We recommend albums,
or films,
or books
that we've recently heard,
seen, or read,
knowing that if we like them,
the other one will too.

Mark's world
grew more constricted
for a while,
as his mom's health grew worse,
but he never grumbled,
never complained,
more than happy
to sacrifice for her
as she'd done for him.

So when she passed on
over a year ago,
he began to expand again,
getting back into writing music,
playing guitar,
and even talking about

traveling north
to visit me this time.
While he has always
sounded upbeat,
he seemed to be
just a little bit happier,
moving forward again,
out of his holding pattern.

Which makes the news
that he passed away suddenly,
a viral infection
that stopped his heart
in between beats,
a musical faux pas
he'd never excuse,
all the more shocking
and fragile.
I still can't believe
that Mark is gone,
that I have to speak about him
in the past tense.
I'm going to miss
our phone calls,
talking about new releases,
what songs
were on our respective radars,
what discs he'd brought home.
I'm going to miss
our discussions
about whether today's music
was better or worse
than in the fifties,
whether the nineties music

had any redeeming value,
whether the last decade
truly has been a renaissance
of amazing films by
outstanding directors.
I'm going to miss
his rants about politicians,
his grumbles about
Schwarzenegger
and other local incompetents.
I'm going to miss
his gentle chuckle
at another one of my puns,
his unwavering support
of my poetry and photography.
I'm going to miss
those every three week
phone calls
that made the times between
so much more bearable.

But most of all,
I'm going to miss
that sweet, soft sing-song tone
at the end of the line,
so happy to hear from me,
greeting me with,
"Hey Peabo."
The passing
of that little joke between us
will haunt me most of all.

HAIKU INTERLUDE

"This place needs music,"
he said. I replied, smiling,
"Yep. Every place does."

SET 2

K-K-K-K-K-Kathmandu

At just before ten a.m.,
this third of September,
in the year 2010,
I have begun my journey
to Kathmandu,
the capital of Nepal,
a city primarily known to me,
as a destination
in song
by Bob Seger,
or the gateway to those
wanting to climb Mt. Everest,
something I don't plan on doing.
Out of all the places
I've travelled in my life,
I would never have guessed
I'd be heading to Nepal,
and then on to Tibet.
Even when I try
thinking about the name
Kathmandu,
it enters my mind
with that stuttering "K,"
just like Bob sings it,
and I'm guessing,
no matter how long I visit,
that tune will keep playing,
my soundtrack
to my adventures in Nepal.

From the Jokhang

At the Jokhang Temple,
considered the heart
of Lhasa, Tibet,
we toured the rooms
and then headed to the roof,
to get photos
of the city
and the Potola Palace.
While quickly filling up
another photo card,
Shena and I
began to hear music,
a work song
similar to the one
we had heard from a distance
at Drepung Monastery
earlier that morning.
Like children
following the Pied Piper's flute,
we began to walk down corridors,
some which we were chased out,
trying locked doors,
going up and down stairs.
We finally found the workers,
singing in unison
as they crushed small gravel
with a large rock
at the end of a stick,
adding water as needed,
to help create a new floor.
We sat,
mesmerized,

listening to the rhythmic thump
of their tools,
with their harmonious song
helping keep time
as work songs have done
for centuries
all over the world.
When one of the workers
offered Shena a chance
to take his place
for a round or two,
she jumped up
and joined in.
I have video to prove it.
Shena's happy to know
that she didn't
mess up their rhythm,
that she's played
a small part
in the restoration
of the Jokhang Temple,
and that she's gotten away
with working in Tibet
without a green card,
though mostly the part
about helping
fix the temple.

Heading South

South of the border.
So far south
we could almost
be north again,
six degrees past
the southernmost city,
getting close
to the Antarctic Circle,
and here in the bar,
on this boat,
still heading south,
the radio plays
all the hits
of the 70s and 80s:
"Tragedy,"
"YMCA,"
"Ring My Bell,"
"Eye of the Tiger."
The drinkers sing along,
until the novelty
and the scotch
wear off,
and they head off to bed,
leaving me here,
to close down the place,
humming along to
"I Love Rock and Roll,"
because I don't want to admit
that I know every word, and
besides,
except for the bartender,
there's no one to impress,

no one to flirt with,
just me,
this poem,
and an empty shot glass.
I'll stay for one more song,
hum along,
and head down to bed
to dream
about how further south
this boat will go.

Mikkelsen Harbor

We awoke
to find fog
still surrounding the boat,
and a part of me fell,
as I knew
we should be close
to Mikkelsen Harbor,
to glaciers,
and penguins,
but all I could see
was gray,
nothingness.
So I bundled up,
and got in the zodiac
to head to shore,
though my hopes
were less than high,
my camera
still deep in my bag.

But then,
like the beginning
of the best technicolor film
you've ever seen,
the fog began to fade
into the most vibrant
blues and whites,
a three sixty
of mountains and snow
and sea.
Though there was no music
aboard the zodiac,

no radio to be found,
I swear I heard a chorus
deep within my ears,
singing Hosanna,
singing Hallelujah,
singing Inglorious,
what a view,
what a day,
and it's only just begun.

Southern Cross (Day 14)

While most people
coming to New Zealand
want to see a Kiwi bird
or Milford Sound,
the one sighting
I was most hoping for
was the Southern Cross,
those four little stars
looking like an upside down kite,
made famous in song.
It's taken almost two weeks,
but finally it's clear enough,
and standing out here,
the wind nudging me back
towards my lodging,
I stare at those stars,
Crosby, Stills & Nash
harmonizing in my ears,
while the other stars
twinkle for attention,
wanting me to know
that they too are special,
that they also
are worth the trip,
but I can't even see them,
my eyes fixed
on those four little
spots of light,
validating
why I came this way,
why I spent the money.
My trip is now complete,

and just in time,
my flight
day after tomorrow.
I could almost close my eyes
the rest of the time,
having also seen
a Kiwi bird,
and Milford Sound,
though I'll keep them open,
just in case.

Octoberfest

Let's face it.
The Germans
aren't particularly famous
for their music,
even though
they did give us
the Scorpions and Falco,
but they are well known
for what they can do
with hops,
which is why I was here,
willing to suffer
through the sing-song
oompah music,
the polka covers
of Beatles classics
only Ringo could love,
all for the chance
to drink
a good German beer
on tap,
fresh.
Though at five bucks a pint,
I'm starting to wonder
if another version
of the "Chicken Dance"
or the "Beer Barrel Polka"
is worth it,
or maybe
I just need
to drink more beer.
A lot more,
I'm guessing.

The One More Pint Band

Saturday night
in a small pub in Laragh,
pints in hand,
excited about what the evening
had in store.
It was our second day in Ireland,
and after a seven-mile hike,
the Guinness was especially smooth.
The football match,
soccer to me,
was just finishing,
Spain beating Russia
1-0.
As the game finished,
the band began.
We were hoping for folk music,
Irish tunes,
traditional songs,
but what we got
was butchered versions of hits
of the 60s, 70s, and 80s.
The Eagles,
Led Zeppelin,
Van Morrison,
Wilbert Harrison, and more
were given the bad bar band treatment,
each song mutated
almost beyond recognition,
almost beyond music.
We continued to drink pint after pint,
hoping that with enough beer,
the songs would become clearer,
the music stronger,

the band better.
After a total of four Guinness,
there wasn't any change,
in either direction,
so we decided to call it a night
before our eardrums exploded,
before our ears began bleeding.
But I do believe we were
only one or two more pints away
from this small band,
in this local pub,
becoming truly mediocre.

Dominique

The plan was
for our first night
in Nashville,
which happened to be
Halloween,
we'd walk on
and around Broadway,
the live Music Row,
and catch some music
jumping from restaurant
to club
to Honky Tonk,
taking in
as much as possible.
After a quick
lay of the land,
up and down the street,
shots of songs
pouring out of windows
and doors,
after checking out
the Country Music Walk of Fame,
after a walk on
the Cumberland Bridge,
reflections of neon skyline
on the river,
and after a quick bite
at Acme Feed and Seed,
we were finally ready
to bar hop,
but as we passed
the Benchmark Bar,

we heard a voice
emanating from a
hot pink and green
dinosaur costume,
or more correctly,
from Dominique Hutchinson,
wearing a hot pink and green
dinosaur costume.
A powerful voice,
confident,
supple,
with just enough rasp
to give it character,
and let you know
she's lived a little.
Singing strictly covers,
from Little Big Town,
George Michael,
Janis Joplin,
and a version
of Dolly Parton's "Jolene"
that would have made
Dolly smile.
We were supposed
to hit more clubs.
We were supposed
to hear more singers,
more bands,
more types of music,
but we stayed there,
in a corner booth,
listening to Dominique
dominate that microphone,
and unlike her costume,

her talent
was far from extinct,
letting us know
right here
was where
we were supposed to be.

I Mean It, Dave, Stop It!

I have stood
on the Ryman stage,
the soul of Nashville,
the original home
of the Grand Ole Opry,
the birthplace of Bluegrass.
I have stood
on the Ryman stage,
trod the same boards
as Bill Monroe,
Lester Flatts,
Earl Scruggs,
Hank Williams,
Dolly Parton,
Garth Brooks,
Bob Dylan,
Bruce Springsteen,
and so many more.
I have stood
on the Ryman stage,
behind the very microphone
Garrison Keillor used
to record an episode
of Prairie Home Companion,
that Mae West
and Orson Welles
spoke to the audience on,
and Minnie Pearl
shouted into, "How-Dee!"
I have stood
on the Ryman stage,
with a guitar

in my hand.
Now I admit,
I did pay twenty dollars
for the privilege,
and it was less than a minute,
but I have a glossy photo
in a cardboard frame
to immortalize
the moment.
Stop laughing, Dave!
It still counts.

I Can't Take It Easy

Andy told me
about his vacation
in the American Southwest,
his stops
at the Grand Canyon,
Lake Powell,
Monument Valley,
hiking in slot canyons,
and driving through Phoenix,
Sedona,
and Winslow, Arizona,
which immediately
put that Eagles song
into my brain,
an endless loop
of the first and second verse,
sandwiching that
oh so hooky chorus,
Glenn Frey and Don Henley
harmonizing like brothers,
and although Andy
talked another five,
maybe ten,
about the second week
of his trip,
his voice
was drowned out
by the broken radio
deep in my skull,
playing that song
again and again,

destined to repeat
for the rest
of the day.

HAIKU INTERLUDE

A good Jazz swing band
has the skills to get even
your kidneys dancing

SET 3

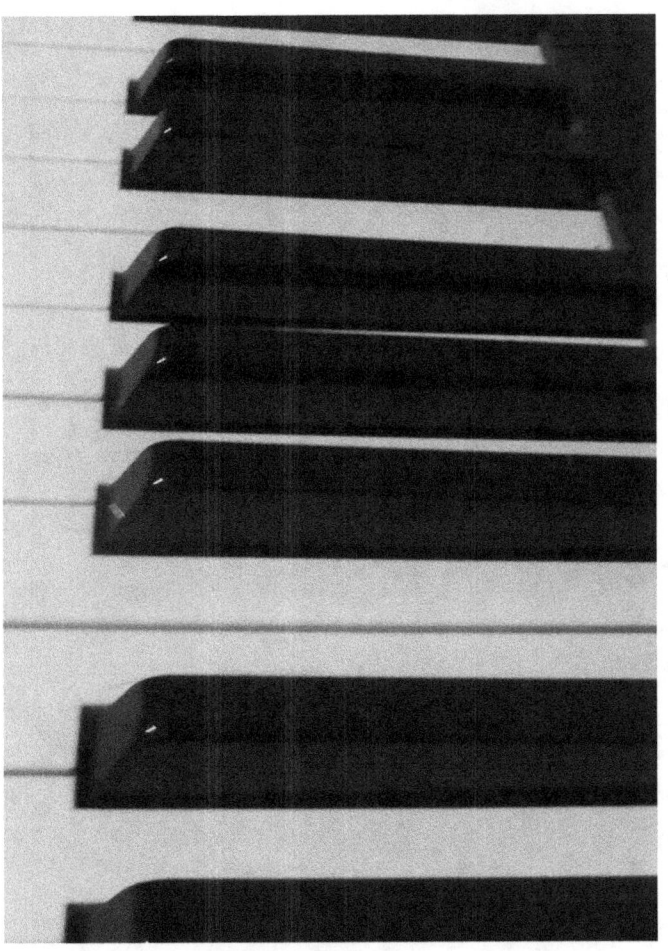

I'm Guessing Fool

When Sarah Vaughan recorded
Gershwin's "Summertime,"
it was April 24, 1957,
not yet Summer,
and her life
had been far from easy.
Did she think George a liar,
or possibly a fool?
Is that why her voice
curls downward
at the end of each line,
finally dropping
below the oboes?
Her mellow tone,
all dark smoke and matches,
suggests that harm may be coming
no matter where
daddy and mama are standing.
Maybe she was hoping,
singing this lullaby,
she could make it all better,
make herself believe
there was no reason to cry,
but she never fell for the lines,
never spread her wings,
never took to the sky.

Thanks Mom

I remember as a child,
my mom playing
Sarah Vaughan's version
of "Summertime"
to help me sleep,
that voice darting out
from the tinny little speaker
of the record player
I wasn't allowed to touch,
her husky alto dancing
with the crackles and snaps,
and I only realized
much later,
that the second verse
was telling me
I would die
and rise up to heaven,
maybe partially explaining
that reoccurring dream
where I'm falling,
waking up
just before impact.

I've Always Liked His Version Better

I heard Kathleen Battle
singing "Summertime,"
her alto
floating, falling
from an open window
overhead.
Her voice
rose above
the traffic and chatter,
and followed me
to the end
of the block,
but as the music faded,
sliding back
into the sounds of life,
I heard Louie
in my head,
continuing the tune,
all gravel rasp
and sly grin,
letting me know
that all was well,
I was safe,
even though
no fish were jumping,
and it was actually Spring.

Being From the West Coast Didn't Help

It wasn't until high school
that I understood
when Billie Holiday
was singing
about strange fruit
swinging from the trees,
it was not
an apple or a pear,
far more sinister,
nowhere near as sweet,
and it was only then
the heartache
in her alto
made any sense,
far too distraught
and forlorn
to be singing
about an orchard of oranges.

Rain Tune

The rain hits the leaves
like a Jazz drummer,
a sweet-natured percussion,
though out of rhythm
to my footsteps.
Or maybe it is I
who is off the beat,
stepping on the half-note
instead of the whole,
a flaw
I blame on my parents.
I must go inside,
out of the precipitation,
away from the weather,
if I'm unable to be
an able musician,
playing along
on today's sad song.

J.C.

Coltrane
was a god,
not the God,
don't be naïve,
but a god
with the ability
to create
with every sigh and moan
of his saxophone,
another universe,
another planet,
each song
a world
upon which we wander,
experience
the sky,
the grass,
the breeze,
walk the paths,
the trails,
which always seem
to lead
to the summit,
each note
a step higher,
each of us
arriving together,
the view
taking our breath,
and we fall
into darkness,
in the silence

between,
until a new world
begins,
our exploration
continues,
our thanks,
our prayers,
made
to a god
who has left
all his creations
behind.

Dave Brubeck, 3/12/06

Dave Brubeck
at the Paramount,
over 60 years
since the start of his career,
more than four decades
since his signature tune.
With his quartet,
he's played for almost as long
as he's been alive,
no breaks needed,
no time outs necessary,
no reason to take five.
As we sat
in the darkened theater,
I leaned into my wife,
her head on my shoulder,
a smile on her face,
her eyes sparkling
like desert starlight.
We will celebrate
our 17th anniversary
in just over two months,
and with our fingers intertwined,
she kissed my neck,
and I wished
at that moment,
that the night wouldn't end,
hoping that
four decades from now,
we'll still be together,
still be as close
as Dave Brubeck's hands,

still making stunning music,
still effortlessly
riding the keys.

Almost Jazz

On this busy street,
there's music,
a dark, sweet melody,
the nine to fivers
moving en masse,
leather soles
and high heel shoes
tip-tapping the concrete,
creating the beat,
a strong, persistent rhythm,
with bass harmony
provided by the crunch
of tires on blacktop,
white walls,
radials,
deep, deep treads,
road crooning.
Riding atop
this musical bed
is the emphatic chirping
of baby birds
in the trees,
crying out
to their parents
for something,
anything,
some wriggly thing,
to fill the hollow.
Or there's the occasional
honk and wonk
of taxi drivers,
and impatient others,

not wanting to wait,
their windows up,
talk radio complaining
about our president,
and the sorry state
of our baseball team,
all of these
a single instrument
in this street orchestra,
yet not a one
able to take a moment,
open their ears,
their minds,
their hearts,
and hear the song
echoing
between the high rises.

Channeling

She knew more about Jazz and Swing,
Gershwin and Armstrong,
but a poem emerged,
pouring from her pen,
all end rhymes and rhythm,
words pacing the cage,
punching and jabbing,
pricking and stabbing,
as she channeled
her inner LL Cool J.
She didn't like Rap,
didn't know any artists or songs,
always changing the radio
when the big bass beat would start,
before the words began.
Misogynistic words,
hateful words,
simple words
that she didn't want to hear.
But there it was.
She'd written a rap.
This gray-haired grandmother,
born and raised in Auburn,
had found her inner gangsta.

Though it scared her,
she wished it could have stayed
longer than a page,
wished she could channel it
whenever she wanted.
The strength,
the power,

the cocksure bravado,
providing new eyes,
style and attitude.
For that grocery clerk
that smirks at her
when asking if she needs help
getting her groceries to her car,
or the poetry group
that only points out her clichés.

But the rapper is gone,
LL has left the building,
nothing on the channel
except a light hiss of snow.

HAIKU INTERLUDE

If Jeremiah
was a bullfrog, the wine he
drank was char-toad-nay

SET 4

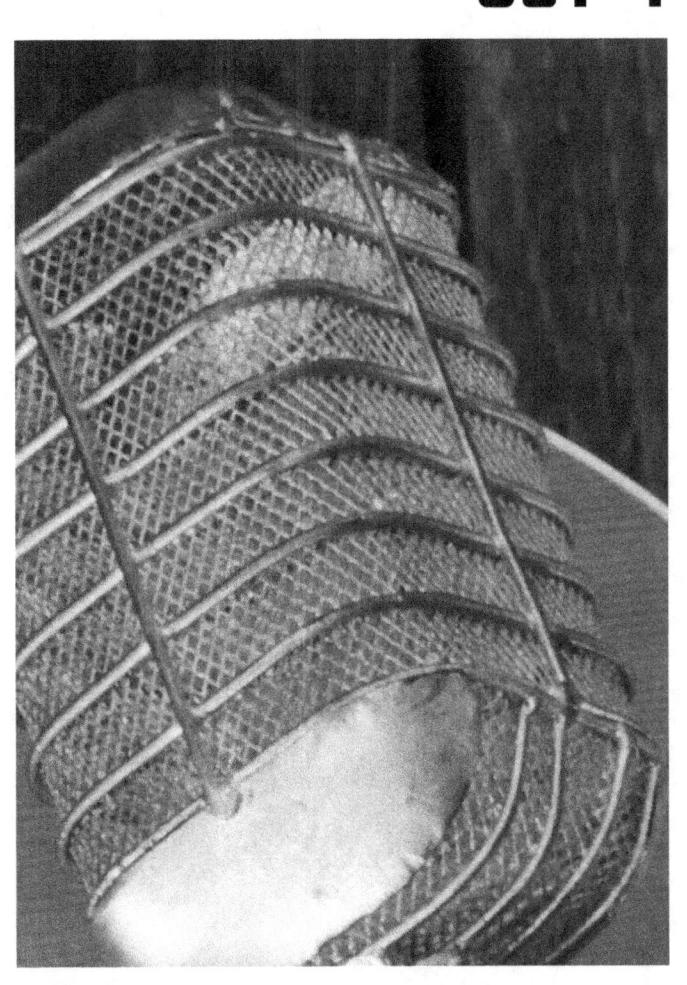

Ponytail Beat

Her hair stuck out
the back
of her baseball cap
like a tail,
bobbing back and forth
as she ran,
a follicle metronome,
keeping time
with her stride.
Earbuds in,
sunglasses on,
she was cut off
from the rest of the world,
yet moving
quickly through it.
She jogged in place
at the corners,
not wanting to stop,
gracefully gliding
back and forth
as needed
to pass pedestrians,
that ponytail
a counterpart
to each move,
left to her right,
right to her left,
yet still keeping time,
keeping the beat
to a song
only she could hear.

Invitation

It is an outdoor concert,
four hundred people,
enjoying the rhythms,
swaying to the groove.
I am in the middle
of the crowd,
one among many,
lost in the show.
That is when
I feel something
grab my hand.

I look down
to see a four year old boy,
black curly hair,
dark creamy skin,
wide brown eyes
staring up at me
and smiling
a friendly grin.

My first thought
is to pull away.
I don't know you.
Who are you?
Why are you
grabbing my hand?
I am a stranger.
Go away.

My next thought
is concern.
Where are your parents?

Looking around,
I see the obvious father,
smiling
that same friendly grin.

I look back
at the boy
and feel remorse
for my innocence lost—
to see everyone
as a possible friend,
to see the world
with rose-colored eyes.
Each event
is new and exciting,
all is safe
and fun.
How quickly it changes.

The boy
tugs my hand
and begins to dance
as only a young child can,
and smile
that friendly grin.

At some point,
those eyes will change,
hardened by the world
and life's tough realities,
but it won't start with me.
I return his smile
and we dance away.

Chile and the Crows

They could have been huge,
should have been huge,
a rock foursome
blending South American rhythms
with Southern Blues,
mixing in
international influences
more than a decade and a half
before Paul Simon
found success with it.
Somewhere,
in my closet,
in a box of 45's,
is a copy
of their one single,
"Half a Nectarine,"
a brooding, folky ballad,
which barely cracked
the Top 200 chart,
number 198
with a bullet
still in the chamber,
and the safety on.
The band broke up
shortly thereafter,
moved on,
went their separate ways.
The Elton John hit,
"Benny and the Jets"
was inspired by
Chile and the Crows,
but he changed the name

for the sake
of the song.
I've heard rumors recently
that Chile's out of rehab,
and they might consider
a reunion tour,
though I doubt
it will ever truly
take wing.
Until then,
I'm going to have to
dig out that 45.

She Doesn't Smile For Me

Hall and Oates were wrong.
Sara doesn't even know
I exist.
Actually, that's not true.
She knows I exist,
as something to avoid,
a sight
she doesn't want to see,
a scent
she doesn't want to smell,
an unpleasantness,
a dark cloud
in her blue sky.
I tried
striking up a conversation,
slipping a note
into her purse,
sending her a vase
full of posies,
but her wall of indifference
is too high a climb
for a scrawny boy
like me.
At times,
I pretend,
when I see her smiling,
it's a sly grin for me,
a possible sign
that she finally sees me,
deigns to recognize
my simple existence,
but then,

she looks my way,
the sunshine
slips behind the gray,
her eyes darken,
her nose wrinkles,
and I shrink back down
and slither away.
Maybe it would
be better for us all
if she didn't even know
I was alive.
Sometimes,
nonexistence is bliss.

Karen

I am the best,
or at least I thought I was
until I met Karen.
She was cheesecake in high heels,
a lilac breeze in winter,
and she broke me in half
like a toothpick
over her nimble ring finger.
We met in a museum,
looking at a fake
statue of David
that reminded me
of a healthy version
of my cousin Gary,
the one that would never marry,
never even meet a girl like Karen.
She would tease me,
and please me,
seduce me
and use me,
and my cries could be heard
from Elm Street
to beyond Third and Main.
She moved quickly,
making me feel
like a tortoise in the sand,
the last leaves on the trees,
as she sped on ahead,
the most likely survivor
on the island,
my torch snuffed out
weeks ago.

The day she left,
or maybe the day after,
Bonnie Raitt cried out,
"I Can't Make You Love Me,"
and I felt her voice crack
in the second chorus,
Michael leaving her too.
I can still smell those lilacs,
taste that cheesecake,
mere ripples in the pond,
tiny vibrations on the earth's crust,
the heat left over from the big bang.

She's Gone

Hearing Hall and Oates
sing those words
over and over again
this morning
on the radio,
seems like
one of life's
cruel jokes,
as if I needed
a reminder
that she's gone.

She collected
the last of her things
yesterday,
leaving me somehow
with less than I started.

The song now segues
into Bill Withers
lamenting
the lack of sunshine
with her departure,
and I'm starting to wonder
if she has somehow
wired my radio
to just be songs
that amplify my torment.

All I know for sure,
is unless Player
is next,
pleading, "Baby Come Back,"
I'm changing stations.

This Song

This song
reminds me of you.
I know you chose it
as our song,
the tune playing
the night we met,
the melody behind
the first time
we made love,
the lyrics feeling
and sounding
like they were
written just for us,
but for me,
this song
reminds me of you.

The piano
reminds me
of your laugh,
all high and light,
the lead guitar
like your personality,
aggressive yet playful,
and the bassline,
oh that deep, throbbing bassline,
is your hips,
especially when you'd wear
that little red dress,
like the sexiest metronome
on the planet,
back and forth,
in perfect rhythm.

Then, when the singer's throaty purr,
suggesting cigarettes,
whiskey,
and honey,
coos about passion,
a small moan
escapes her throat,
and I can feel
your breath in my ear.

And there,
right there,
as the song begins to fade,
when the saxophone kicks in
out of nowhere,
like the melody
of another song,
a howling
haunting honk
of loneliness and despair,
this part,
and only this part
reminds me of me.

That Song

I heard that song today
on the radio.
That one
you said was ours.
That one
that caused you
to run out and buy the CD.
That one
that whenever it came
over the radio,
you'd turn it up
and look me in the eye
and sing
as loud as your voice would go,
damn the tune,
or whether you knew
all the words,
except it had love
and forever
in the chorus.

Too bad
we didn't even make it
to the third verse,
let alone the final fadeout,
which is my favorite part.
You know where it's going,
you're comfortable with it,
and you don't want it to end.
But it always does.
I heard that song today
on the radio,

and I changed the channel
before she got to the chorus,
before I could
remember the words.

I'm No Angel

She had bought me
Madonna's *Like A Virgin*
because she said
the song "Angel"
reminded her of me.
We only dated
for about 4 months,
and while I never
truly understood what she meant,
when I hear that song now,
almost two decades later,
it makes me smile
and think about
what might have been.

My Linda

I do not have a band.
I don't even play guitar,
but I would like to know
if you would be my Linda
and I could be your Paul.
John and Yoko
got the attention,
all the headlines,
but nobody writes
about all their time apart.
Paul and Linda
were always together.
He created a band,
and made her a member,
touring as a couple,
though she really couldn't play.
They shared
in each other's joys
and sorrows,
and he held her hand
and sang quietly to her
as she passed away.
Now I know
it's a strange request,
as we are already married,
and I realize
that I do not have a band.
I don't even play guitar.
But I would like to know
if you would be my Linda
and I could be your Paul.

HAIKU INTERLUDE

The singer told the
crowd he didn't do requests,
unless he was asked

SET 5

The Opening Band

Nobody pays attention
to the opening band.
Tonight,
it's Johnny Slim.
It doesn't matter
how great he plays guitar,
or that his fiddle player
is playing so hard
her bow looks like a horse's tail.
The audience
is just biding their time,
waiting for the headliner.
There are hundreds of conversations,
almost drowning out Johnny Slim.
Like the two ladies
talking about the guy
they saw at the mall
who was drop dead gorgeous
and had a cute butt.
Unfortunately,
he had a big zit
on the left of his nose,
but it's nothing
a little Noxzema couldn't cure.
Or there's the guy
telling his buddy
about how work totally bites
because his boss is an ass
and he's way underpaid,
but he's just waiting
for the economy to pick up
and then he'll find another job

and tell his boss to go to hell.
Johnny finishes his set
and when the headliner
takes the stage,
the crowd cheers,
and grows eerily quiet,
waiting to hear that hit single
that's at the top of the charts.
Their only hit single.
Shaking his head,
Johnny vows someday he'll have a hit,
because nobody pays attention
to the opening band.

Open Mic

Auburn Coffee Shop,
Open Mic Night,
the guitarist
strumming Bob Marley,
his mouth moving,
but all the words
forced through
his nasal passages,
a high pitched whine
Bob could hear
six feet down,
thanking his lucky stars
that he was already dead,
his songs
now being butchered
while baristas
make lattes
on a Saturday night.

Aural Oatmeal

Jesse Sykes and the Sweet Hereafter
performed at McCaw Hall
on a rainy Sunday night,
twelve songs that never got faster
than a waltz step,
a dozen servings of aural oatmeal,
all warmth and comfort
that left me wanting a nap,
or at least a soft pillow.
Even her vocals
strained to rise above a whisper,
sung like secrets,
sweet nothings
in a lover's ear.

The drummer
seemed to move in slow motion,
the drumsticks hanging
between light taps
on the snare and cymbal,
not wanting to disturb,
not wanting to wake someone up,
or cause a need for earplugs.

Maybe it was the venue,
the stormy weather,
or the fact that it was Sunday night,
something was keeping their show
mellow and non-threatening,
which is more than I can say
for the rain outside,
playing a much faster song,

an up-tempo rhythm,
a nice quick beat,
but no one paid a penny
to watch it perform.

Late Tuesday

It was Friday night at the Tractor,
but it was Late Tuesday on stage,
a local band,
made up of three female singers,
and two nondescript guys,
one on bass,
the other on drums,
behind the stage lights,
strictly backup.
The lead guitarist
was a long-limbed, gawky,
flip-haired, Gidget blonde.
The pixieish, pigtailed
Susanna Hoffs look-a-like
was the best singer of the three
and also played keyboards,
while the third,
a girl next door,
long-haired chubby sister,
played keyboards too,
though only one set was needed.
Their harmonies were strong,
in a Bangles, Expose
kind of way,
but my eyes kept being drawn
to the four foot ten, short-haired,
lawn tractor capped brunette,
wearing an "I Love Late Tuesday" t-shirt,
staring dreamily at the band,
especially at pixie girl,
with that moon-eyed silly grin
I remember seeing on my sister

as she flipped through
her latest issue of Tiger Beat.
I half expected to see
cartoon hearts
circling her head,
as she looked sighingly stageward.

I don't mean to be
condescending or catty,
though I must admit
a hint of jealousy.
I've always wanted to be
on the Tractor stage,
a large crowd shimmying
to my words,
a young lady up front
staring dreamily my way,
but poets don't have groupies,
don't draw large crowds,
never cause an audience
to shimmy or sway,
lucky to get their spouse
or best friends to show up
unless they promise to buy dinner.
It may not be a big club,
this band may not sell
a lot of records,
but tonight,
they make me wish and hope
for bigger things,
maybe a fan or two,
or someone willing to wear
an "I Love James Rodgers" t-shirt.

The Paperboys

I've known Tom
for over twenty years,
have seen
the Paperboys perform
so many times
I've lost count.
Over forty
for sure,
likely over fifty.
There has been
a semi-consistent rotation
of other members,
with Tom the constant,
at least five cute female fiddlers,
though the most recent one,
Kalissa,
will likely stick around
for quite some time
as Tom married her.

There are members I miss,
Hanz, Steve, Shannon, Cam,
Shonda, Kendel, Paul,
so many more,
but on the mic,
it's always Tom.
It's his band,
his personal mix
of Celtic,
World,
Country,
Pop,

and Bluegrass,
swirled together,
stompy music,
sing along
at the Tractor Tavern music,
dance
in front of the stage
at an outdoor venue music,
more and more
each year
my kind of music,
an aural warm blanket
of comfort,
love,
and a pint of beer.

Tom just posted
on the band's website
their summer dates,
so I'll be adding on
one more show
to my total.
I may not know
how many times
I've heard "She Said" live,
but I can always count
on a blissful night.

A Chance To Dance

She was six foot tall,
wearing a hot pink cowboy hat
and matching boots.
Not a normal color
for western attire.
In between,
she wore a thin,
spaghetti strap,
yellow sun dress,
probably purchased
at a local thrift store
for under six bucks.
On her face,
she wore a sheepish grin
that went well
with the hat,
and her eyes danced
to the music.
She was obviously not
looking for men,
hanging seductively
on the arm
of a short haired gal
in blue t-shirt
and suspenders,
but men
were definitely
looking at her.
Almost every guy there
asked her to dance,
and dance she did,
western swing,

waltz,
and the two-step.
I think
she would've danced the Charleston
if the music had been right.
She was having fun
and so were the guys,
a moment of eye candy
draped on their arm,
to not be judged
for their looks or their weight,
just if they could dance,
and dance they all did.

Encore

We're all out here,
in the darkness,
stomping and screaming,
cheering and clapping,
the band having finished
their main set,
now just off stage,
the two guitarists
enjoying the control,
the adulation,
while the bass player
and the drummer
take this moment
to chug another drink,
do another line,
and just at the moment
that our volume,
our enthusiasm,
begins to ebb,
they jump back on stage,
perform three more hits,
the songs
we were all hoping for,
paying for,
praying for,
and then the lights pop on,
the band pops off,
and the encore
is no more.

Balance Due

When the fire broke out
in the nightclub,
another case
of pyrotechnics gone wrong,
as people ran for the exits,
ran from the flames,
ran to escape,
the bouncers blocked the door,
sending people back to the bar,
back into the fire,
to pay their tabs,
a reverse of their usual job
of not letting people inside.
When the smoke
became unbearable,
the bouncers stepped aside,
letting everyone out, but
by then, it was too late.
Over three hundred perished
in the fire,
most from smoke inhalation,
and I wonder
how many of those
are no longer here
because they owed twenty bucks
to a business
going up in flames,
the cash and receipts
also lost in the blaze.

HAIKU INTERLUDE

When Bill sang, "Ain't no
sunshine when she's gone," he must
not have known Trudi

SET 6

The Song's Incorrect

The song on the radio
may be proclaiming
that it's beginning
to look a lot like Christmas,
but as I peer
out the window
at the brooding grey sky,
dulling and muting
even the most vibrant of colors
into flat blandness,
nothing out there
makes me think
the holiday's only
three days away.
While you can't miss it
in the mall
and department stores,
out here
there's no decorations,
no lights,
no sale signs
and tinny holiday tunes
over the sound system.
A friend told me
that there's a rumor
going around,
that we could get snow,
which would definitely
make it look
more Christmas-like,
and would make the DJ's choice
of "Winter Wonderland"

a lot more fitting,
but I think those whispers
of the white stuff
are just wishful thinking.
Christmas may be coming,
but outside my window,
it's beginning to look
like just another Tuesday,
which wouldn't make
much of a carol,
I must agree.

Blanket of Song

It was a blue sky day,
temperature in the eighties,
sunblock on the nose,
blanket on the grass
kind of Saturday.
We were at an outdoor concert,
an L.A. band called Quetzal
exposing us Northwesterners
to what they called "Chicano rock."
As Martha and Gabriel
traded vocals back and forth,
their voices in perfect harmony,
I was taking photos
and grooving to the music,
while my wife rarely looked up.
She was listening,
but her focus
was on the baby blanket
she was knitting for your child,
due in the Fall.
She would argue
she was just multi-tasking,
making the most of her time,
but I digress.
As her needles clicked,
moving the loops of yarn
back and forth,
they began to click
with the rhythms of the songs,
and she could feel the music
becoming more solid,
feel the wave of tones

lapping at her toes,
then her knees,
and she began to worry
she'd be washed away
into their musical sea,
but the multiple notes
started to catch
in the weave of the blanket,
the song intertwining with the yarn,
until she had caught it all,
like a fish in a net,
and she could see the music
was now part of her knitting.
So as you unwrap it,
it may just look
like a small, pastel baby blanket,
the perfect size
for the child carrier,
but when you wrap it around
your baby,
they will hear
a quiet lullaby,
their heart beating
in time with the drum,
and they will be warm,
protected,
surrounded by song.

Naked Support

When Vince suggested
that we go to the Strip Club,
Wes and I readily agreed.
We said to ourselves,
and to our spouses,
that we did it for him,
to support him,
recently divorced,
the single one of the group.
But what we thought deep down
in our brain was,
"Yeah, an excuse."
So there we were,
three middle-aged men
ogling the nudity,
watching the scantily-clad girls
walk by,
all flirting with Vince.
We'd put him on the aisle,
closest to the ladies,
closest to the action,
or inaction
unless you have money,
and even then,
it's simulated action.
But Vince didn't mind
and Wes's head kept swiveling,
trying to take everything in
all at once,
like a man who'd been dieting
finally allowed
to step up to the smorgasbord.

Personally,
I was enjoying the music.
Now don't get me wrong.
The girls were beautiful,
the video playing on the monitors
similar to ones I'd rented before,
but the choice of song
each dancer chose
was what interested me most.
"Sex on Wheels."
"Gett Off."
"Shakin' That Ass."
All great songs
that made sense.
But why did the dirty blonde
choose Paul Simon's "Graceland?"
I would have agreed to a lap dance,
if she had offered,
just to ask her that question.
At least,
that's what I tell myself,
and my wife.

Everyone's A Critic

When the red
and blue lights
pull up
behind your car,
and the officer
walks up
to your window,
three songs
you should not
have blaring
from your stereo are:
John Mellencamp's
"The Authority Song,"
Sammy Hagar's
"I Can't Drive 55,"
and NWA's
"Fuck the Police."
They are not fans.
But the one piece
that will result
in an instant ticket
is Bobby McFerrin's
"Don't Worry, Be Happy."
I'm not sure
exactly why,
but every officer
I've ever met
hates that tune.

Reading Billy

I've spent
most of the afternoon
reading a new book of poems by Billy Collins,
while Robert Johnson,
George Thorogood,
and Otis Rush
cry the Blues
in the background,
the cat curled
deep into my lap,
deep asleep,
in a position
only a cat
can find comfortable.
As the shadows
grow longer outside,
I begin to feel guilty
wasting another Sunday.
I consider
putting the book down,
getting up
to make dinner,
take the laundry
out of the dryer,
make my lunch
for work tomorrow,
and at that moment,
the cat shifts,
burying her nose
a little further underneath
her left front paw,
another long exhalation,

and I smile,
adjust my reading glasses
one more time,
and turn the page.

Sing It, Sam

On another Saturday night,
sitting quietly,
an autobiography of Bob Newhart
resting in my lap,
Sam Cooke's
"A Change is Gonna Come"
drifts from the speakers,
his smooth as Belgian chocolate voice
telling me to relax,
forget about the recent turmoil,
and troubles at work,
it will all be okay,
a change is gonna come.
And while I love his sound,
a true tenor
with a tone so pure
it couldn't be
anything less than a miracle,
I'm finding it hard
to be comforted.
While I do believe
that a change will come
someday,
with all of the changes
thrust upon us
over the last six months,
I'm not completely sold
it will be for the better.
The song slowly fades,
and I smile,
as Sam begins to croon
about not knowing much

about his schoolwork,
and I have to agree
that if you love me too,
this will be
a wonderful world,
at least for now.

Steve

His voice
is equal parts
honey and sunshine,
sweetness and warmth,
and when he
infiltrates my headphones,
my ears
are thankful
for the gentle intrusion.
I own
all his solo recordings,
though there aren't many,
spending most
of his time now
producing,
supporting,
recording others.
On my I-pod,
all songs
are carefully selected,
painfully scrutinized,
no weakness,
no chaff,
yet every so often,
his acoustic guitar
chugs and thrums,
his tenor
flitting effortlessly
over the chords,
and I bump up the volume

each and every time,
sometimes hitting repeat
once or twice,
just because I can.

Sitting in the Car

On a Sunday without sun,
rain lightly tapping
on the windshield,
I sit here waiting,
now 45 minutes in,
waiting for her
and her friends
to emerge,
so we can truly
start our day.
As if echoing my feelings,
Bruce Cockburn
softly strums "Pacing the Cage"
from the tinny
factory-installed speakers,
and when Richard Thompson
begins singing the story
about the "1952 Vincent Black Lightning,"
even though
no one has returned,
by the last verse,
I want to start up the engine
and just drive away,
looking for
a Red Molly of my own,
but the radio
goes to commercial,
with ads
about tonight's television shows,
so I sit here and wait,
hoping another great song,

or my lovely wife
and her friends,
come along soon.

I Think I Love Her

She wore a black beret,
not a raspberry one
like that girl
in the Prince song,
and her chapeau
wasn't found
in a second hand
or thrift store.
Not a chance.
This looked new,
high-end,
haute couture,
or as haute couture
as a beret can be.
We didn't talk,
no eye contact,
no interaction at all,
just a gal
across the room
with a nice hat,
but if I could,
I would thank her
for unintentionally
pushing play
on the tape deck
in my mind.
I do love that song.

Song in My Head

There's a song in my head,
deep inside my skull,
imbedded,
ensconced,
stuck.
I don't know
exactly how it got there,
or when,
but luckily,
it's the whole song,
all four minutes and 11 seconds
of the live version
of the Talking Heads'
"Burning Down the House."
Usually,
when a song
goes on endless loop
in my brain,
it's a snippet,
a line or two
of the chorus,
over and over,
ad nauseam.
So the whole song
on repeat
is okay for now,
and while I'm standing here
on this mountain,
deep snow all around me,
David crooning about arson
somehow makes me feel
just a little bit warmer.

Oh Heavenly Day

Outside my window,
it's raining lightly
from an endless sky of gray,
while in here,
I lounge lazily,
Patty Griffin singing
"Oh Heavenly Day,"
her voice
haunting my speakers,
slow and low.
The song
gradually builds
in momentum
until by the end,
singing along,
with conviction
and passion,
I start to think
that despite the weather,
maybe this truly is
a heavenly day,
and I need
to stop wasting it
and get outside.
But first,
at least for now,
I better grab
my heavenly raincoat.

Long Way to the Top

Waiting for her,
I'm here
in the parking garage,
window down,
breathing in
exhaust tainted air,
AC-DC screaming that it's
"A Long Way to the Top
if you want to Rock n' Roll."
I'm only on level two,
as there were
no parking spots below,
and my job,
and my writing,
don't seem to be
getting me to the zenith
anytime soon,
so it's not just Rock n' Roll
that requires
such a torturous journey
to reach the peak.
But as her train arrives,
I see her face
staring out
the rectangular window,
smiling my direction,
and I realize
I'm right
where I want and need to be.

Always Drumming

He drums with his thumbs
every waking moment,
on any surface
he can find,
from tables,
to armrests,
steering wheels,
and even peoples' heads,
though usually,
it's someone he knows.
Sometimes there's music,
though many times there's not,
just the constant
tippity-tip-tap of his thumbs,
keeping the rhythm
to his hours,
days,
and years.
And all of this
would be fine
if he was a drummer,
or even
strictly a musician,
but he's not,
and he can't even
keep a good beat.
I kind of hate that guy.

Just Listen

Standing
next to her mother,
four years old,
uneven pigtails,
swim goggles,
striped top,
polka dot fleece pants,
pink tutu,
mismatched socks
and shoes,
swaying and twirling,
softly singing
to herself,
while Mom
stands still,
staring hard
at the light
at the crosswalk,
as if this somehow
will make it change
any quicker.
Mom grabs
daughter's hand,
roars, "Stop it!"
one more time,
while her daughter
continues to spin,
continues to sing,
not able to comprehend
how or why
her mother can't hear
the song seeping out

from all around them,
enveloping them,
embracing them,
whether they want it to
or not.

HAIKU INTERLUDE

I wish you were here…
Oh, sorry, not you. I was
just singing Pink Floyd

SET 7

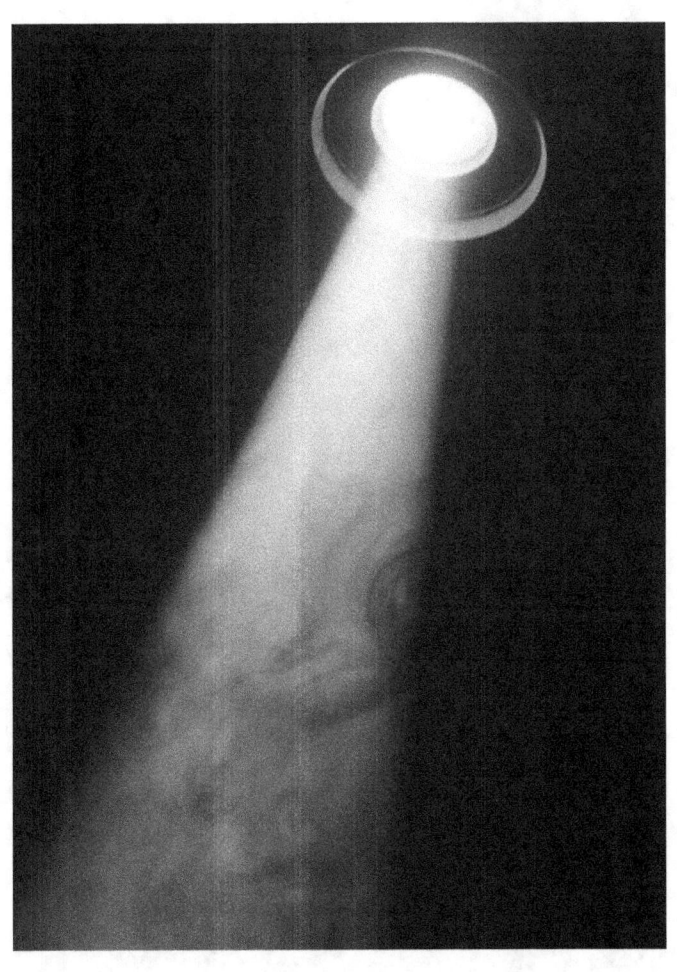

Can't You See the Tears?

Whenever it rains,
I can hear,
blaring from a tiny speaker
deep within my grey matter,
Stevie Ray Vaughan lamenting,
the sky is crying,
and I still can't get over,
now 25 years later,
hearing about his helicopter
hitting the side
of a mountain,
gone forever,
my generation's Buddy Holly,
and as the song builds
to its final chorus,
I lift my face
towards the heavens,
and let the tears
fall around me.

Fallen

I heard Scott Weiland
had died
while I was driving
in the darkness
towards work.
He was found dead,
passed away in his sleep,
on his tour bus
in Bloomington.
No cause of death
was reported,
but even the casual fan
of Stone Temple Pilots
or Velvet Revolver
knows it was drugs.
His addictions
had plagued him since
the nineties,
more than two decades
of searching,
aching,
needing
to fill the hole
in his arm,
in his body,
in his being,
never succeeding, until
last night,
while he slumbered,
when he fell
into that open pit
like Alice.

But there will be
no Wonderland,
no Mad Hatter,
no Cheshire Cat,
and I hope,
for his sake,
no Queen of Hearts,
screaming "Off with his head,"
as he's been
through enough.
Let him rest, Queen,
please,
let him sleep!

Bowie

"Space Oddity"
was my introduction.
I was six,
maybe seven,
already a music junkie,
and this song
was the first
I'd ever heard
where you didn't know
the end
of the story,
as ambiguous
as the singer
was androgynous.
From that moment,
I snapped up
each and every album,
following him
from Ziggy Stardust
to the Thin White Duke,
through the Brian Eno trilogy,
the hugely successful
Nile Rodgers record,
all of it.
He never
chased the hits,
never pandered,
always experimenting,
always taking us
on a new journey,
always leading the way.
Now that cancer

has written
his final song,
the Starman
has returned to space,
and the stars
look very different
today.
Planet earth is blue,
so I'll put on
my red shoes
and dance the blues.
Will you join me?

The Gospel

You were neither
preacher or profit,
no religion,
no church,
merely a singer
in a band,
but we
were your disciples,
poring over
every album,
every song,
every lyric,
to try to understand,
to feel closer
to someone
who seemed to understand
us.
But then,
deep into the night,
as so many of them do,
too tired
to go on,
you stepped
into the abyss
and you were gone.
Now,
with clarity of hindsight,
we again
pore over
every album,
every song,
every lyric,

old words
take on new meanings,
leaving us
with so many questions,
too many questions,
including,
should we follow?

P.R.N.

He played
every instrument
on his first two albums,
but except for
"I Want to Be Your Lover,"
I rarely listen to those.
I discovered Prince
with the *Dirty Mind* album,
number three,
two before
1999 put him on the charts,
and one more
before *Purple Rain*
made him a superstar.
Being a teenager,
I thought
the songs on *Dirty Mind*
and *Controversy*
were naughty,
sly,
subversive,
unlike anything else
I'd ever heard,
and just funky enough
to make this
scrawny white teenager,
who couldn't dance
if he tried,
want to boogie.
Over thirty-nine total albums,
some better than others,
Prince grew up,

found religion,
married,
divorced twice,
performed at the Super Bowl,
and sold millions of records,
all while keeping
that sly,
subversive,
dirty mind.

Hearing this morning,
nonchalantly,
from a co-worker,
that Prince is dead,
passed away
in an elevator
at 57 years old,
I can't fathom
this world,
my world,
without his creative,
naughty self
making more music.
There will be
no more concerts,
no more new songs
(besides the labels
rushing out
all the thousands of tunes
Prince supposedly
has locked
in the vaults

of Paisley Park),
no more controversy,
no more dirty mind,
and the part
that hurts me most,
the thought
I cannot quite comprehend,
is when we finally do
live to see *The Dawn*,
he won't be there
to see it with us.

No More Frank Zappa in This World

I've been surprised and bewildered
by the change in our climate.
Not the rain,
or lack of snow,
the slow increase in temperature,
though those are disturbing.
No, it's the puritanical
leanings,
the laws of the blue states,
fearing flesh,
scared of sex
on the television,
afraid it's replacing
all of the violence,
which is just harmless fun.
I tried to blame the president,
middle America,
and narrow-minded people,
but I realized
they're not to blame.
The balance had shifted.
There is no more Frank Zappa in this world.

That hairy square peg musician
is now raising a crop of dental floss
on another plain,
a different Montana,
worldly weasels no longer
ripping his flesh.
He battled the borders
and the shackles
placed upon our freedoms,

a squeaky wheel
that wouldn't take the grease.
And then,
way before his time,
way before our time,
way before the fight was over,
he lost a different battle,
and no one has picked up the gloves.

Before the bell sounds
at the end of round fifteen,
someone needs to step in the ring,
to correct the balance,
because
there's no more Frank Zappa in this world.

George Jones

I heard on the radio
that George Jones
passed away today,
the last
of the country crooners,
the last
of what I call
"Grandma Country,"
the style of music
my grandmother listened to
before she herself
left the airwaves
a few years ago.

She called it,
"Real Country,
not that bubblegum crap
they try to pass off
as Country now."

I always thought
George had a smooth voice,
but most of his songs
were so slow,
and a bit boring for me.
Yet Grandma loved
to hear him sing,
and from what I've heard,
he enjoyed singing,
and sadly enough,
in both cases,
I have to make those statements
in the past tense.

From James to Jimi

I was only four
when Hendrix passed,
never got to see him live,
feel every change
of guitar string
deep inside my chest,
never felt the heat
from the flames
coming from his guitar,
never stood
in a crowd,
hundreds deep,
each and every person
leaning forward,
as if being pulled
towards the stage.
I've only heard him
on vinyl and CD,
watched grainy videos
from Woodstock
and the Isle of Wight.
I own every album,
even the "new" material
released by the family
three decades after
he stopped recording.
I sing along,
though I never have
been experienced,
never truly,
so it always feels
like I'm lying

to his memory
when I harmonize
to his caramel tenor,
"I have!"

Out of the Garden

Though they were
invisible
to everyone else,
Chris could see
the demons
all around him,
circling,
taunting,
chiding,
always just out of reach.
Alcohol and Oxycontin
didn't make them
disappear,
but they were calmer,
quieter,
almost silent.

He started a band
that played hard
and loud,
where he could be
out front singing
in a haunted howl,
and when the drums
and guitars
were fully amplified,
and he closed his eyes,
the demons would
disappear
for a while.

When the record hit,
and fame came calling,
money just allowed
for more expensive drugs
and top shelf booze,
but the demons still danced
just out of reach.

With the help
of friends
and family,
he tried sobriety,
cleaned up,
and the demons kept dancing,
yet almost imperceptibly,
day after day,
began to get closer.

In Detroit,
just before
another show,
as he was waiting
to take the stage,
the demons
got close enough
to touch him,
burn his skin,
hiss in his ear,
and even though
the band played
louder than ever,

he could hear
the demons
taunting,
chiding,
laughing.

A few hours later,
when paramedics found
his lifeless body
hanging in the bathroom,
they swore
they could smell
the scent of sulfur
on the rope.

He Was Our Man

Everybody knows
the songs of Leonard Cohen,
songs of love and hate,
songs from the road,
songs from a room
inhabited just by you
and his words.
His lyrics,
though personal,
contained popular problems,
old ideas,
new ideas,
the past,
the future,
various positions,
opinions,
and the dark,
dark truth.
You want it darker?
Turn out the light.
Bow your head,
drop to your knees,
and sing "Hallelujah"
to the heavens,
for today
marks the death
of a ladies' man,
the tower of song
lies in rubble,
this world,
this room,
now silent.

HAIKU INTERLUDE

Some like Crosby, some
like Stills, some like Nash, and some
are forever Young

SET 8

It Better

In the darkened theater,
Carly's alto sang in Dolby how
"Nobody Does It Better,"
then the movie started,
and although I've always
liked James Bond,
when the lights came up
I had to disagree with her.

A Star Is Born

Her voice
is like a barbwire fence,
her tone
like the liberty bell
after the crack,
and she carries a tune
like a musical sieve,
but Annie P. Johnson
has always believed
she was born to sing.
Anyone who's heard her
would call her deluded,
or at least deaf,
but Annie knows
she's a natural singer.
She feels the music
tapping out a rhythm
all along her capillaries,
her feet constantly dancing
in her shoes.
Deep, deep down,
she knows
there's a singer inside her,
a song within,
and until the world
is ready and willing
to hear it,
she sings it,
quietly crooning,
just below her breath,
like a musical whisper,
her secret
safe for now.

Five Verses about the Park

She was singing,
loud and off-key,
a tune only she knew,
though similar
to "Mary Had a Little Lamb,"
except with made up lyrics
comprised of all the events
of her day.
She may only be
three years old,
with no work,
no meetings,
no major appointments,
but by the time
she was done
singing her song,
all nineteen minutes
and thirty-six verses,
including three on grilled cheese
she'd had for lunch,
I was surprised
how busy her day had been,
and by comparison,
how empty mine was.

She Had a Growl

Her voice
was as clear and warm
as a Caribbean sky,
and all attention hung
on her lyrical hooks.
But she had a growl
that she used for emphasis,
that made me stare
even when I tried to look away.
A low rumble,
a husky howl,
a pack-a-day grumble
that takes genetics
or years of neglect
to cultivate.
She didn't use it often.
She kept it in her pocket,
next to her picks,
ready to be played
when she needed it.
It was sensual,
and sexual,
dark and cool,
but I wouldn't want it
aimed at me
when she used it in anger.
It had power
when sedentary,
let alone
when it curled up
and pounced.
She's almost done

with her set now,
the opening act,
preparing the audience
for the main event,
but unless their lead singer
also has a growl,
for me,
the show's already done.

Hers Was the Voice

Hers
was not the voice
of a sixteen-year-old
pop strumpet,
singing the latest
cotton candy ditty.
Hers
was the voice
of forty years of living,
of passion
and heartache
and tears,
all leaving their tattoo
on her vocal chords.
She sang traditionals
and contemporary tunes,
brushing every story
with her personal eye for detail,
her personal voice of experience.
The pub,
usually a din
of conversation
and commerce,
beer drinking
and laughter,
was so quiet tonight,
you could hear a jaw drop,
and every time
she opened her mouth,
many did.
Hers
was not the voice

of an everyday singer
in an everyday bar.
Hers
was the voice
I wish you had heard.

(I'm not) Walking on Sunshine

I hate that song!
"Walking on Sunshine,"
that one-hit wonder
piece of bubblegum fluff,
the most used song
on movie soundtracks,
the go-to ditty
to connote euphoria,
is the one song
that makes me cringe
more than any other,
and there are plenty
that make me shiver.
I swear,
each time it plays
on the radio,
where it seems to be
on regular high rotation,
a small part of me dies,
a brain cell shrivels up,
and another angel
never gets his wings,
condemned for eternity,
like me,
in a hell
where the only song playing
on a constant loop
is by Katrina and the Waves.

Killer Star Tattoo

She has a killer star tattoo
on her right shoulder,
usually hidden under sleeves,
but visible
on those rare occasions
she wears a dress.
The star's a reminder,
a souvenir,
of her days in a band,
Faster Tiger,
like Sleater-Kinney
without the success,
though she still believes
they should have been bigger,
they should still be performing,
they should still be making records,
they should not be working
a nine to five job,
in a cubicle,
under fluorescent lights,
dressed in business attire
that hides your
killer star tattoo.

Sara Hickman

Sara Hickman
sings in a warm tone
about love and life,
like a musical Mom,
wanting you to bundle up,
look both ways
before crossing the street,
and enjoy her songs
like chicken soup
for your ears.

I own at least
a dozen of her recordings,
have listened to her
for longer than
either she or I
would want me to admit,
and have always taken comfort
in her sweet alto
and clever lyrics.

After finally
catching her live
just last year,
her smile
that I'd seen
so many times
frozen on my CD cases,
made me feel
related.

She hugged me,
during intermission,
like a lost son,
and she made me
feel found.

You can keep
your Godfather of Soul,
and King of Pop.
Sara Hickman
is my musical mother.

Everybody's Looking for Something

I love Annie Lennox.

I was hooked
the moment her fist
came down on that desk
as the first percussive beat
in the "Sweet Dreams" video,
the camera panning up
to her wildfire
of short, cropped hair,
a men's business suit
making her somehow
look more masculine
and feminine
at the same time,
her voice
both seducer
and punisher,
sin and heaven
in an amber honey alto.
And when she sang,
"Some of them want to use you,
some of them want to be used by you,"
I wasn't sure
which side I was on.

After all these years,
I still don't know.

Shining Star

Star Anna,
hair dyed the blue
of a Midwestern dawn sky,

sings confessional rock songs
in a small pub
on a Saturday night.

She wears a black hat
like the one
Jimi Hendrix used to wear,

thick black brim all around,
so when she bows her head
over her guitar,
she hides her face completely,

the painful introvert
chanting over and over
inside her head,

"They can't see you."
"They can't see you."
"They can't see you."

She says
very little
in between songs,

only looks up
a half dozen times
the entire two hours,

tries to be hidden,
camouflaged
while under the spotlight,

not fully understanding
that with each lyric,
each song,

we can catch
little glimpses,
hints of
who she really is,

her vulnerable invisibility
making her
so much more

interesting,
captivating,
beautiful.

Madonna Behind My Eyes

Recently, ready to rest
I closed my eyes,
and there in the blackness
was Madonna's face,
circa *Desperately Seeking Susan*,
smiling bemusedly at me,
as if she was supposed to be there,
or was about to tell me
a really good joke,
or was just amused
by my surprise
at seeing Madonna
in the darkness
behind my lids.
I waited for a few moments
to see if she would speak to me,
or sing,
or something,
but she continued to just smile.

So, I opened my eyes,
rebooted the night,
and tried again,
and when my eyelids dropped,
she was gone.

Since then,
I've wondered
why she was there,
why she was smiling,
and what that joke
might have been.

Emily

Believe it or not,
Neil Young used to have
a small British woman
growing out of his back,
providing hindsight,
insight,
and wizened perspective
to his daily life.
She'd been back there
throughout his career,
giving him song ideas,
looking out for lawyers
and record execs,
letting him look back
on where he'd been.
He had her removed
in an elaborate surgery,
in Stockholm, Sweden,
in the early 80s,
and his music,
and career,
have suffered ever since.
The song "Old Man"
was actually written by her
and originally titled "Old Woman,"
but Neil changed the gender,
to avoid confusion,
and keep the spotlight
off of her.
Although known by family
and friends,
as Emily,

Neil worked hard
to make sure
she was never seen
onstage,
or in public.

Caught on film
only once,
she's forever frozen,
in black and white,
on the cover of
After the Gold Rush.
If you ask Neil about her,
he'll deny it,
act like he doesn't know
what you're talking about,
but if he removes his shirt,
which he seldom does,
you'll see the scar
where Emily used to be,
a part of him,
that he wishes
was still there,
still helping,
still seeing,
still watching his back.

Not Quite Dolly

She looks a little
like Dolly Parton,
with less makeup,
less rhinestones,
and less breasts,
but more than
a passing resemblance,
so everyone she meets
breaks into "Jolene,"
or "9 to 5,"
or "I Will Always Love You,"
and every gray haired,
bearded gentleman
within a ten-block radius
belts out "Islands in the Stream"
when she walks by.
And the sad part is,
she doesn't even
really like Dolly Parton's music.
She prefers the blues,
like Robert Johnson,
or Blind Lemon Jefferson,
or even B.B. King,
but unfortunately
she doesn't look like
any of them,
so wherever she goes,
the soundtrack to her life
is an endless medley of
off-key renditions
of Dolly's greatest hits.

Anyone's Muse

She's a fairly plain,
nondescript,
middle-aged woman,
eating a sandwich
as if she hadn't
had a meal in a while.
Her clothes are bland as well,
tan shoes,
tan pants,
and a gray hoody sweatshirt,
the word "MUSE"
in large black letters
across her chest.
A reference,
I'm guessing,
to the band,
as I truly doubt
she's anyone's muse,
truly doubt
she'd inspire
great works of art,
truly doubt
anyone would
write about her
in story,
song,
or poem.
Wait.
Well, I'll be damned!

Lynn Marie

That gal
could sure work a room.
She was skinny,
with blonde hair so tousled,
men tried
to hand her a comb.
It was no surprise
that everyone was staring.
Besides being beautiful,
she was playing accordion
and leading her band
through polka music
for an alternative world.
She had smiles
and energy
to give,
and she did so
throughout her set,
using her body,
eyes,
and accordion
to flirt with
every guy in the place.
We loved
every wink,
every grin,
every touch
she threw our way.
By the third song,
we were all
just keys
on her instrument.

What Are You Thinking?

What are you thinking
while you are singing
up there on the stage,
eyes closed,
holding the microphone
like a safety blanket,
or a fellow conspirator?
You seem to return to us,
between songs,
after the applause,
to tell us a story
or thank us for listening.
But as soon as the music starts,
your eyes close,
and you are gone again.
Are you thinking about groceries,
or the long bus ride,
the seedy motel where you're staying,
the cute guy in the front row
mentally undressing you?
Are you undressing him too?
At times,
you seem to smile a smile
that only you recognize,
and I doubt
you're going to explain it
between tunes.
Are you afraid of us?
Are we uglier
than last night's audience?
Why do you close your eyes?
What are you thinking

while you are singing?
That's the song
I want to hear.

Karan Casey

Her voice
was purer
than the whiskey
at the bar,
and her songs
caressed my ears
like a lover's kiss.
She sang of death
and murder
and misery,
in tones that made them all
sound pleasurable
and pleasant,
until I was
enjoying the anguish
in her tales.
She could harmonize with the birds
like Snow White,
and lull a young child to sleep
all while singing about drownings
and stonings,
stabbings
and love gone wrong.

As I grow older,
all I ask in life
is whenever tragedy strikes me,
I want to hear about it
in a melody
sung softly to me
by Karan Casey.

Kake King

She was barely five feet tall
and the guitar
was almost bigger than she was,
dwarfing her body,
dwarfing her hands
as she strummed,
and picked,
and plucked,
and pounded,
making notes I didn't realize
a guitar could make.
For this outdoor show
it was still too early
to turn on the spotlight,
but there on the stage,
she was already shining.

Patty Smith Is a Beautiful Woman

Patty Smith is a beautiful woman.
You won't see her
walking a runway,
or on the cover of Vogue,
hawking cosmetics to the masses.
Her beauty
radiates from the stage
as she snarls into the microphone,
her gaunt face and body
tense
with the power
of the music and words
pulsing through her.

Patty Smith is a beautiful woman.
Her convictions,
her pride,
and her love
of the rhythm of words
mixed with music
keep her going.
She could have stopped,
multiple times.
She had great reasons.
But not even
the snuffing of the lights
around her
left her in darkness
for long.

Almost thirty years later,
she can mesmerize
and energize

and truly surprise
the largest of crowds.
In a stadium of thousands,
she'll make you feel
like you're standing beside her,
her words
meant for only you.
And as you stand there
taking in her message,
you realize
Patty Smith is a beautiful woman.

HAIKU INTERLUDE

Lionel Richie's wrong—
Sunday morning's not easy,
Saturday night is

SET 9

Arlo

If he had known
that people would still cheer
at it's opening chord
forty years
after he wrote it,
that he'd perform it
over ten thousand times
throughout his career,
that it would be
the one song
that he would be remembered for
even though
he's written hundreds,
he never would have recorded it.

It was meant as a joke,
a lark,
a rambling protest song
nestled into a silly story
about being arrested
for littering.

Eighteen and a half minute
guitar tunes
with spoken word verses
are not likely pop songs,
not likely top 40 hits,
not likely tunes
to be played every Thanksgiving
on thousands of stations
precisely at noon.

But here he is
four decades later,
plucking this same song,
singing the same words,
wishing he'd written
something grander,
like his father,
wishing he'd written
something wittier,
wishing he'd written
something shorter,
only content in the knowledge
that the constant residuals
have allowed
all of his other
worldly wishes to be answered.

Dan Bern

Dan Bern
is performing tonight
in a record store.
He usually plays
much larger venues,
but his friend
owns the place,
so here he is,
with a small crowd
interspersed
among the racks of CDs
sitting on crates of vinyl.

Dan doesn't strum.
He pounds the guitar
as if it were
his own bare chest,
speak-singing
with that nasal snarl
that's become the calling card
of all
modern folk singers.

He packs lots of words
into his lyrics,
and they come at you quick
and hard,
like blows from a prize fighter,
which is fitting
considering the size
of Dan's biceps.

I think he could whip
any folk singer out there,
whether in the ring
or just arm-wrestling.

Everyone's paying
rapt attention,
intimidated into doing so,
fearing that
if you're not listening,
he just might reach out
and smack you.

I'm Busy

Every time
that Bob Marley sings,
"No Woman, No Cry,"
I want to point out
he was happily married,
and it is better
to shed tears of love
than not to cry at all,
but I'm far too busy
singing every word,
as loud as my voice
will let me.

In Bloom

In his cover
of their song,
he strips it down,
removes all the color
from every corner,
the angsty, angry reds,
the despondent blues,
repaints it
using lighter shades,
more yellows and greens,
splashes of orange,
until this sound painting,
this aural flower,
seems new,
original,
unique,
and it's only
when the chorus arrives
that those familiar words
remind you
of the band
that recorded it first,
though never distracting enough
for you to miss it.

His Music Is Still Timeless

The last time
I saw John perform
was over twenty years ago,
a small club
in the basement
of a classic car dealership
in Tacoma,
and there was less
than fifteen people
in the entire place,
including John
and the sound guy.

This show tonight
has greater attendance,
somewhere near
a hundred people,
musician and crew excluded.
His accordion work
is still flawless,
lightning fast when needed,
slow and lamenting
as the tune requires,
but I was most
taken aback
by his hair,
now a silver-gray helmet,
no blonde remaining.
It was slightly awkward
talking to him afterwards,
getting him to sign a CD
from thirty years ago,

his boyish face
grinning from the booklet,
now so much older,
especially since,
by what I can tell,
in all that time,
I haven't aged
more than a day,
possibly two.

AC/DC Done?

Rumors
are swirling about
that AC/DC
is calling it quits.
No more albums.
No more tours.
I missed it.
I will never be
shook all night long,
never drive the
highway to hell,
never have my
dirty deeds
done dirt cheap.
I had opportunities
to see them live,
but I squandered them,
thinking there would
always be next year.
I have to hope
the rumors aren't true,
and if they do
turn out to be fact,
maybe someday,
if I'm lucky,
they'll reunite
before we're all
back in black.

But Which Kind of Science?

When Thomas Dolby
sings that song,
instead of
blissfully singing along
to the happy, poppy beat,
I've always wondered
exactly how
she blinded the singer.

Did she use chemicals,
work up a test tube
of a concoction
of her own creation?

Did she test
light density
on different cloths
until she found one
that would make
the perfect blindfold?

Did she study
microorganisms,
discovering one
that deteriorates
human flesh
she could apply
to the inside
of his glasses?

Did she force
his eyes open

with toothpicks,
and use
high-powered lasers
to fry his retinas?

Did she create
the perfect
pointed instrument,
made out of some new
lightweight
titanium composite,
and then
just jab him
in the eye,
at least twice?

I know
these are completely
gruesome and horrible thoughts
running through my head
due to
an 80s pop song,
but Mr. Dolby
sounds just
too damn upbeat
for a man
who's just lost his vision.

Not Thin

A guy
just came into the restaurant
who looks exactly
like that singer
who had a huge hit
on the pop charts
last summer,
an earworm of a single,
based on the melody
of a Marvin Gaye song.
I think he got sued
by the estate,
but I never heard
if he had to pay
the family or not.
While I loved the original,
this "new" song
left me cold,
feeling uninspired,
all the way
from the borrowed bassline,
to the shallow lyrics,
and ending with the video
of the naked girls
walking back and forth
as he leered on.
He has a decent falsetto,
but I don't think
that he's very talented,
likely just a one-hit wonder,
but I would like to know
if that's really him,

here in this restaurant,
and if he'd sign an autograph,
for my friend,
of course,
not for me.

We Can't All Be Dylan

All artists,
whether writer,
painter,
musician,
all of them,
want to be Bob Dylan,
the world changer,
the innovator,
with a nearly
six-decade career
so far.
Though everyone
conveniently forgets
the motorcycle accident,
and I guess
since he lived,
it's okay to do so.

But if you haven't
completely reinvigorated
your genre,
been seen
as the new Messiah,
and a Judas,
before you're thirty,
it's too late
to be Bob Dylan.

I'd be happy
to even be
a one-hit wonder,
celebrated

for a short moment,
my one poem
living on and on
in collected volumes of verse.

I'd even be fine,
since I'm way past
being Bob,
being soul singer
Charles Bradley
who hit it big
with his debut album
released at age 62,
only to lose his life
to cancer at 68,
a few years of glory,
a little afterglow
before the end.

Not quite as good,
but still okay,
would be
to be like singers,
discovered after they die,
their talent revealed,
enjoyed,
and mourned for the loss.

But all of us artists,
while we want to be Dylan,
would accept
any of the lesser options,

every one of us
fearful
we'll live
and die
in obscurity,
our life's work,
our passion,
moldering in an attic,
or a city dump,
slowly disintegrating,
disappearing,
gone.

Stop Believin'

I don't care
what Steve Perry keeps singing
over and over,
sometimes you need
to stop believing,
give up,
and move on.
I know,
it's a catchy song,
and he sings it
with such urgency,
it's easy
to want to give in
and keep on believing,
but we all know
how that worked out.
Steve left the band,
had one hit single,
and disappeared
into mushy ballads
and limp rock songs,
and the band
did even worse.

Even though
they are no longer together,
all parties involved
seem to keep on believing
that against all odds,
the hit singles,
the glories and accolades
will keep on coming.

They don't see
that it's all behind them,
gone.
And god how I envy them
for not seeing it.

No Discussion

It's one of those days
where I'm not
in a very chatty mood.
I don't want to discuss it,
explain it,
argue it,
or talk about it at all,
making me think about
that Rod Stewart song
that always made me laugh.
If Rod didn't want to
talk about it,
then why in heck
was he singing about it?
Maybe it was easier for him
if it had a tune.
but not me.
I don't want to warble it,
harmonize it,
or sing it acapella.
If I could spend
the rest of the day
with my mouth shut,
exalting in the blissful silence,
without a dozen offers
to talk about it,
I might be able
to begin tomorrow anew,
ready to converse,
blab on and on,
and maybe even gossip a little.
Maybe.

but until then,
like Rod says,
I don't wanna talk about it.

Morning Song

It was still early,
so I crept silently
down the hallway,
or as silently
as a big guy like me can,
and closed the door
to the bathroom.
Obviously,
one of the kids
was already awake,
had taken a shower,
as the tub
was still wet,
and droplets
from the shower head
were beating a consistent
insistent rhythm
on the ceramic below.
Before I knew it,
almost unconsciously,
my heel
began a bassline
on the tile,
and my fingers
tapped the sink.
I started to sing,
low and quiet,
still not wanting
to wake the others,
and the words
came pouring out,
like someone

had forgotten
to turn off my faucet,
a song
I had never heard,
but was now
confidently belting out,
the usual bathroom acoustics
making me sound
far superior
to what I should.
As I slid
into the last chorus,
I could hear harmony
from behind the door,
a few "aah, aahs"
and "baby, babys,"
and when I reached
the inevitable conclusion
to my tune,
I stopped,
just the drip, drip, drip
rhythm remaining.
I then heard my brother-in-law
tell me
if I wiggled the knob
the dripping would stop,
and with that,
the music ended,
and it was
just another Saturday morning
in Vancouver,
except there was now
a line

waiting to get in here,
and all I wanted to do
was continue to sing.

HAIKU INTERLUDE

The trombone told the
Jazz man, "You can play me, but
don't give me no lip."

SET 10

It's Too Late

Why do they sing
"Take Me Out to the Ballgame"
in the seventh inning
when you are already there?
I understand
it's a fun song.
I get
it's tradition,
but no one
would logically ask someone
to take them somewhere
they already are,
and have been
for multiple hours.
I could sing
"I Am Here at the Ballgame"
or even
"Please Bring Me Back to the Ballgame,"
though I
wouldn't sing it
with as much enthusiasm,
but as is,
I can't do it,
won't do it.
Be happy
if I'm willing
to hum along,
but since you're up,
when the song's over,
I really would
like some peanuts
and Cracker Jacks.

The Leafblower Symphony

The November rain
is in the air,
and the leaves
are on the ground.

Walking across campus,
the drops
beat timpani
on the concrete,
as my footsteps
keep the rhythm.

My natural percussion
is soon joined
by the low drone
of the leafblower symphony.

Three landscapers,
red hat
on bass blower,
yellow shirt
on tenor,
and overalls
on high falsetto.
Their power tools
in perfect pitch,
the three-part harmony
would make Pavarotti,
Domingo,
and Carreras
humbled and envious.

Our song,
a fine accompaniment
to this blustery day.
Grooving
to this natural tune,
oblivious
of the pothole,
until I hit it,
twisting my ankle
and joining the leaves
on the ground.

The rhythm stops
and the leafblowers
power down,
as red hat,
yellow shirt,
and overalls
rush over
to see if I'm okay.

Embarrassed,
wet,
a little sore,
but not broken,
I get back up,
and continue on
down the path.
The leafblowers
start anew,
but the harmony's gone

and the beat
is all wrong,
the song
lost forever.

Disappointed,
I round the corner
to hear
four more landscapers
rhythmically raking.

Sounds of the Sound

Sun slowly setting
on Orcas Island,
a beer
out on the deck
with Mike,
soaking in
the last few rays,
relaxing,
talking about life.
In a break
in the conversation,
we just listen
to the light breeze
tickling the branches,
the waves
roaring to shore,
then gurgling,
burbling,
over the rocks
on their swift return home,
the squonk
of the Canada geese,
the occasional call
of the cormorant,
the shrill shriek
of the seagull,
children laughing
and giggling,
playing in the sand
just out of view.
As the soft harmonies
join together,

a melody to nightfall,
suddenly
the loud voice
of a young girl,
maybe five or six,
screaming,
"GET THE BUCKET!
GET
THE
BUCK-
ET!!!"
Then nothing,
even the ocean
shocked into silence.

Dream On

Ever since she heard
her favorite musician
was on tour,
and at every stop
would bring one or two
folks on stage
to play his guitar
or sing with him,
she'd been practicing
every day,
working out
the chord progressions
to every song,
singing in the shower
and during her commutes
to and from work
no matter how many others
were on the bus.

She dreamed
almost every night
of the band
moving to the bridge,
and how he'd lock eyes
with her,
reach out his hand,
she'd join him on stage,
and perform so well
he'd divorce his wife,
move in with her,
where they'd duet forever.

So, when the concert
finally arrived,
she put on
her favorite dress,
sat in the front row center seat
she'd spent
two month's salary on,
and when the bridge began
on her favorite song,
and he reached out
to the lithesome blonde
four seats over,
the one with less talent
in her entire size zero body
then she had
in one chubby finger,
she felt the final wisps
of her dream
float away
like it does
every morning
when she opens her eyes,
though this time
was different.

She wasn't sleeping,
but this wake up
was painful,
and just as
she felt the tears
begin to infiltrate
the corners,
he looked down
and smiled at her,

that big goofy grin
she'd fallen in love with.

It was only a moment,
and she's pretty sure
he was looking at her,
letting her know,
telepathically,
it would all
be okay,
keep dreaming,
he'd be back
on tour again
when the new album drops,
and besides,
this will just give her
more time to practice.

Music Lover

She said
she loved music.
She said
she owned lots of CDs
and still had
plenty of records.
Yet she didn't know the difference
between Neil Diamond
and Neil Young,
Boston and Chicago
were strictly cities,
Moby Grape
was a fruit juice
for kids,
and Eminem
was just candy
that didn't melt
in your hands.

She didn't know
the name of the band,
or the title of the song,
none of the words,
or even a semblance
of the tune,
but it was her favorite song.
She had twenty dollars
ready to spend,
and was now staring at me,
expectantly,
hoping I'd pull the song
out of the air,

like a rabbit
from a top hat.

But I'm no magician,
and she thanked me for trying,
went on with her day,
whistling,
way out of tune,
a song
only she knew,
though not well enough
to say
what it was,
or who sang it.

Big D

In the divorce,
he gave her the house,
the land,
the car,
the truck,
everything
but the guitars,
amplifiers and mixers,
cases and stands,
his music.

She considered
trying to take those too,
but since she had
cheated on him,
there was just enough
guilt mixed in
with her hatred,
she was willing
to give him that.

He vowed
never to marry again,
no matter the woman,
or how strong the love,
not willing
to ever again
gamble on the chance
of having to give up
even one nylon string.

Stop Writing Songs

Frustrated
and numb
from the daily onslaught
of bombings
and stabbings,
shootings
and death,
he thought,
"What were his songs
really doing?"
He'd written thousands,
but nothing had changed.
Well,
that's not completely true.
Things seemed to be
getting worse.
So he pulled out his pen,
a black Bic
with a cushioned grip,
and he wrote
one last song.
He said that was it.
He was done.
He would write no more.

What he didn't realize
was he didn't control it.
It's not a spigot
you can just turn the handle on,
not a switch
you can flip,
or curtains you can drop

on the darkened stage.
Within an hour,
another song came,
and there's been hundreds more
since then,
and still nothing's changed,
except he's switched pens,
and stopped
watching the news.

More Like a Steel Sieve

It's starting to seem
that each and every day,
the older I get,
the more I forget.
Since my brain
only has so much space,
so much memory,
it can't hold everything
it's bombarded with,
and it must be
near capacity.

I imagine a little guy
running around
inside my head,
dusty boxes
and file cabinets all around,
and he's pulling files,
shredding paper,
deleting memory
from my mental hard drive.

But he seems to be removing
the wrong stuff,
leaving the trivia,
like who recorded
the original version
of "Spirit in the Sky,"
or who remade it
in the 1980s?

Those are still there.
But the names of my neighbors,
or my pin number,
seem to keep disappearing.
No steel trap up here.

In fact,
I'm starting to worry
that I may have written
another poem
a lot like this one,
maybe even better,
though I can't
remember for sure.

But I can tell you
who were the two stars
of the film
All the Right Moves,
in case you're interested.

HAIKU INTERLUDE

Like an old record
player that lost its needle
I can't find my groove

encore

It Won't Sing "Freebird"

This is not
a rock-n-roll poem.
You will not
have to lock up
your daughters,
hide your liquor bottles,
or plug your ears.
This poem
will not snarl
or howl,
scream
or cry.
This poem
will not die young,
burn out,
or go back out
on the road
sixty years later
on its fifth annual
farewell tour.
This poem
is not strung out
on vodka and heroin,
never snorted cocaine,
never shotgunned beers
until it blacked out,
or spent the night
in a bed
full of groupies.
This poem
doesn't have groupies.
This poem

doesn't have fans.
This poem
only knows one song.
This poem
knows at least three chords,
and the truth,
but when it's done,
it will leave the stage,
the spotlight will dim,
and it will not
return for an encore.
This is not
a rock-n-roll poem.

Artistry

There's a black and white photo
of an acoustic guitar,
framed,
hung on the wall
of a coffee shop
near my house.
The image
is stark,
simple,
a close-up
of the strings,
a bit of the body,
and you can see,
if you look closely,
a crack in the wood,
and I swear,
every time I pass it,
every time I see it,
I can hear
a low strum,
a sweet harmony
that's no longer perfect,
not quite on pitch,
yet still
making a melody
that echoes
behind the glass.

SHOW'S OVER, FOLKS!

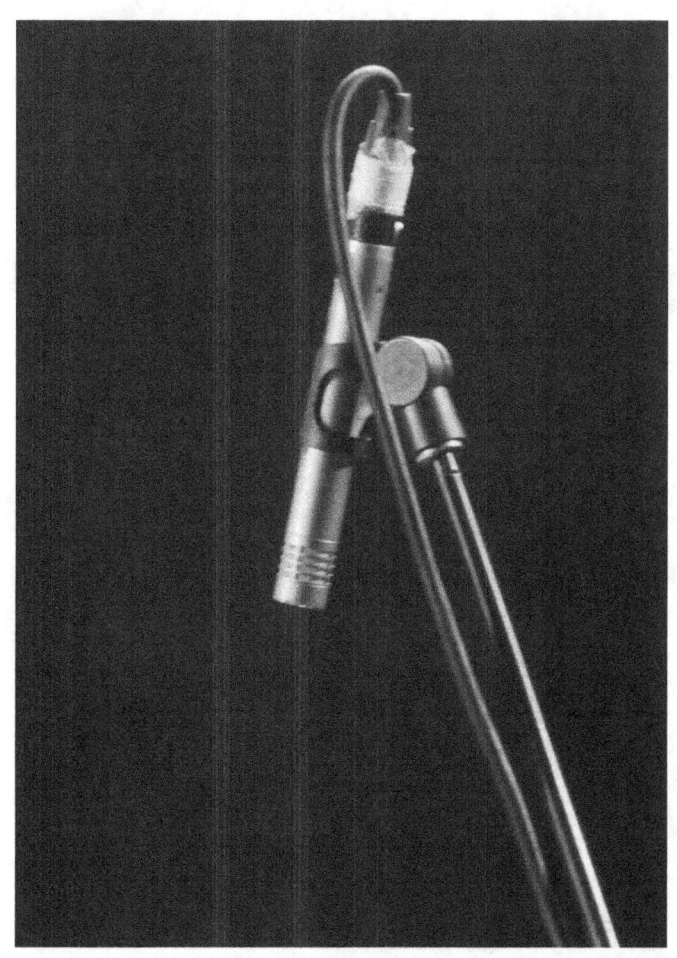

GOOD NIGHT

About the Author

James Rodgers is a prolific poet living in Pacific, WA for more than two decades, and has been in the Pacific Northwest his entire life. He lives with his very patient wife and two very psychotic cats. While James prefers humor, he writes all kinds of poetry, with a focus on music, humor, kids, travel, and so much more, along with many song lyrics waiting to have music attached to them. He also created his own humorous style of haiku that he calls haikooky, and you can see his blog at: jamesrodgershaikooky.blogspot.com. All the haiku included within this volume were originally published on jamesrodgershaikooky.blogspot.com and you can read hundreds more of them there.

James has three self-published chapbooks, and has had poems published by *Prism Magazine, Ha!, Poets of the Kent Canterbury Faire, Fly By Night Press, WPA Members anthology, Wrist, Washington English Journal*, and many more. He was also the winner of the WPA Charles Proctor Award for Humor in 2005. He has been rejected by *Raven Chronicles, Prairie Home Companion,* and *45th Parallel,* among others.

Along with poetry, James is an award-winning photographer, having won multiple prizes in Auburn's annual photo contest. He has had multiple art shows of his work, provided the black and white images used in Cindy M. Hutchings book *Tree Talk,* and the tulip portion of the collage cover for Brendan McBreen's book *Cosmic Egg,* both published by MoonPath Press.